COMPOSING BRIDGES

An English Translation from the Chinese Edition

MAN-CHUNG TANG

China Communications Press Co., Ltd.

Beijing

Preface

This book displays in pictures the bridges I designed in China from 2002 to 2011. It was a very gratifying nine years!

China has built many spectacular bridges during this period. I am very fortunate to be able to participate in this historic construction boom and to design some of these bridges. Most of the bridges I designed are in Chongqing, a city in mid-western China that is often called by engineers the "Bridge Capital of China", because it has more major bridges than any other city in the country.

I was born in Guangdong, China in 1938 and left the country in 1949. I came back to visit China for the first time in 1979 when it was opening up, after three decades of seclusion. I opened an office in Chongqing in 1994 and I received my first bridge design contract in 2002.

Having designed bridges in all six inhabited continents in the world, it is really exciting to be able to design and build bridges in my homeland. The first Chinese bridge I was commissioned to design was the Caiyuanba Bridge in Chongqing. Since then, I have been fortunate to have the opportunity to design the many bridges contained in this book. Some of them are currently being designed and some of them are under construction; some of them are already opened to traffic; and two have been placed on a waiting list by the Owner after completion of the design. All designs are based on the Chinese design codes, but, in special cases, also consulted US, European and Japanese specifications.

Bridge design is an art. Each bridge has its distinctive topography, culture, economic and political requirements, and restrictions. Therefore, every bridge is unique. The experience of designing each bridge has been valuable. In this book, I will explain the reasons and the context for each design choice. For example, why did I use a rectangular box shape for the arch ribs of the Caiyuanba Bridge and not the popular round steel tubes? Or, why are the two arch ribs in the Dagu Bridge not the same? Why is the pedestrian walkway of the Jiayue Bridge placed under the deck? I hope this explanation will be especially useful for younger engineers.

"A picture is worth a thousand words." Pictures are the best way to explain the structure of a bridge. Therefore, I will provide as many pictures as possible. The readers can enjoy the beauty of the bridges and understand the bridge structure at the same time.

China has built many types of bridges. Innovation is encouraged and aesthetics is always a priority. We have emphasized these two virtues in all our bridge designs.

My experience in designing these bridges has been most exciting! China is a good place to work. The people are friendly, reasonable and more people-oriented. It is a dynamic society. So, designing bridges in China is fun! I enjoy every minute of it!

Man-Chung Tang (邓文中)
May 2011, Chongqing, China

CONTENTS

Bridges Opened to Traffic

Caiyuanba Bridge — Chongqing — 003

Second Shibanpo Bridge — Chongqing — 023

Dagu Bridge — Tianjin — 037

Second Wujiang Bridge — Fuling — 054

Sanhao Bridge — Shenyang, Liaoning — 067

Jiayue Bridge — Yuelai, Chongqing — 081

Yuyun Bridge — Yingkou, Liaoning — 097

Tuojiang First Bridge — Luzhou, Sichuan — 104

Taijiang Bridge — Sanming, Fujian — 108

Fujiang First Bridge — Hechuan, Chongqing — 116

Bridges Under Construction

Nanping Bridge — Hechuan, Chongqing — 124

Twin River Bridges — Chongqing — 130

Huihai Road Bridge — Lianyungang, Jiangsu — 144

Second Yangtze River Bridge — Changshou, Chongqing — 152

Jialing River Bridge — Caijia, Chongqing — 156

Bridges Designed But Not Built

Guangli River Bridge — Dongying, Shandong — 164

Dongping River Pedestrian Bridge — Foshan, Guangdong — 170

Bridges Opened to Traffic

Caiyuanba Bridge

Location: City of Chongqing, over the Yangtze River.
Main span: 420m.
Two levels: Upper level, six lanes of highway;
 Lower level, two monorail tracks.
Bridge opened to traffic on October 29, 2007.

Caiyuanba Bridge · Chongqing

Caiyuanba Bridge in the foreground, Shibanpo Bridge in the background

Chongqing is a city in the mid-western region of China with a population of about 32 million. The City is, for the most part, mountainous. It is bisected by several big rivers: the Yangtze, the Jialing, the Wujiang, and the Fujiang. Development of the area requires the construction of many major bridges. In 1981, the City saw the completion of its first major bridge, the First Shibanpo Bridge over the Yangtze River, a multi-span prestressed concrete girder bridge with a main span of 173m. Since then, the City has completed many bridges. Today, Chongqing has the most major bridges in China. Hence, it is often called the "Bridge Capital of China".

The metropolitan district is divided by two major rivers, the Yangtze and the Jialing, into three parts: the southern district, or Nan'an; the Central District, or Yuzhong Peninsula; and the northern district, or Beian. Caiyuanba Bridge is a link between Yuzhong and Nan'an. It is in the heart of the town and is about 1.2km upstream from the First Shibanpo Bridge. It carries six lanes of city traffic on its upper deck and two tracks of monorails on its lower deck. The 420-meter span was the world's longest arch span for dual highway and rail traffic when it was opened to traffic in 2007.

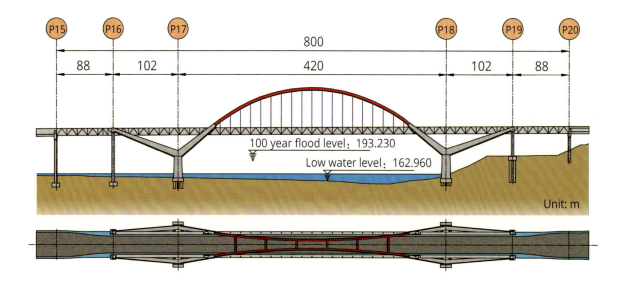

The entire project was significant. Besides the tied-arch main spans, there are the southern and northern approaches, the Sujiaba Interchange connecting the main bridge to the southern shore, and the Caiyuanba Interchange connecting to the northern shore. The main span length was determined by the Waterway Department of the Ministry of Transport based on the navigation requirements in the area. The 420-meter navigational clearance is much larger than that of Shibanpo Bridge because it is located on a curve in the river.

The bridge is very visible from most parts of the town. Aesthetics was an important factor in the design. During the preliminary design stage, various bridge types—cable-stayed, suspension, arch and truss bridges—were studied. But the general public and the City preferred an arch bridge.

Aesthetic lighting of the bridge

It was exciting to have the opportunity to design a bridge in China after having worked on bridges in every inhabited continent in the world. I was born in this country and had hoped for such an opportunity since I began my career. I had previously reviewed the designs of and acted as advisors for several other bridges, such as the Nanpu Bridge, Yangpu Bridge, and Humen Bridge. Designing this bridge was different in that it was my first Chinese design. And, it is especially so because the bridge is in Chongqing, a beautiful city that I dearly love. I studied the landscape and the history of the City to develop the bridge concept. I am happy that the bridge is now enjoyed by the citizens.

A few times, I took a taxi to the jobsite. When the taxi driver found out that I was the designer of the bridge, he told me that I did not have to pay the fare because he loved the bridge!

What a great satisfaction for an engineer!

The bridge at night

The City of Chongqing is rather hilly. The landscape is very graceful. I used to compare Beijing as a seriously looking Mandarin, Shanghai as a talkative merchant, Wuhan as a muscular worker, and Chongqing as a beautiful lady. A bridge in such a landscape should be as slender as possible. This led to my selection of the basket-handle tied-arch bridge, with uniform arch ribs.

The water level of the Yangtze River at this location may vary more than 30m, which requires special considerations for possible barge collision and corrosion protection. An arch with its arch ribs partially submerged in water would not look good! So, I raised the arch high above the normal water level to rest on four vertical concrete columns; in that way, it is above the highest level of water. I used concrete for the lower portion of the bridge because concrete would fare better in case of a possible barge collision; concrete would also be more resistant when submerged in flood waters.

Aesthetically, the concrete frame makes the bridge appear sturdier.

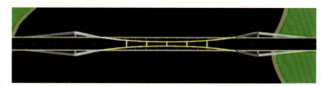

Each of the arch ribs lies in the same plane as the concrete "Y" frame. The two planes tilt slightly inward to form the basket-handle configuration.

COMPOSING BRIDGES

China has built many concrete-filled, steel tube arches. This type of arch was also seriously considered as an alternative to the box shape arch ribs. However, a concrete-filled steel tube arch would have looked too bulky at this location.

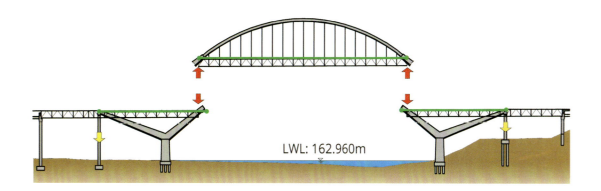

Under permanent load, the structural system of this bridge can be treated as a simple, tied-arch bridge resting on two concrete "Y" frames. All three ties can be individually stressed to achieve the best internal force distribution.

Caiyuanba Bridge · Chongqing

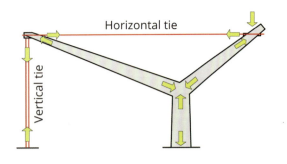
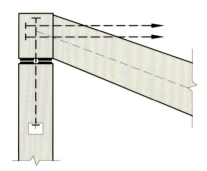

Each tie is comprised of several groups of individually sheathed and epoxy-filled seven wire strands. Each strand can be replaced individually, if necessary.

Each concrete "Y" frame has two ties: a horizontal tie and a vertical tie-down at the end. The global bending moment can be eliminated by properly adjusting the forces in these two ties.

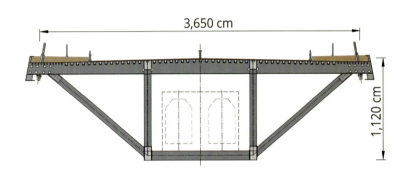

Trapezoidal girder and side spans without vertical struts

The girder is about 12m deep to provide enough room to accommodate the monorail on the lower level. Typically, this type of girder would look very bulky over the river. Making it into a truss made it more transparent. A truss also offers the monorail passengers a more open view of the river. In addition, the trapezoidal-shaped cross section of the girder makes it look much slenderer.

The hangers are anchored to the girder at both edges at the juncture of the floor beam and the diagonal strut. The hanger force can be divided into two components: the horizontal component goes to the floor beams and the vertical component is carried by struts.

The in-plane buckling of an arch bridge depends on the combined stiffness of the girder and the arch rib together. Hence, the arch ribs of this bridge can be made very slender because the girder is very stiff.

The stiff girder also allows the deletion of all spandrel columns on the side spans. Those spandrel columns are typically used to support the girder. This greatly improves the openness of the bridge.

The bridge is a popular passageway from Yuzhong to Nan'an

Color Selection

Chongqing is famously called the "fog city". Although most industries have been moved outside of the City, public buses are using natural gas instead of petroleum. Still, the humidity from the two rivers cannot escape from the river valley, and it is still foggy most of the time.

The yellow and the orange-red are the two most visible colors in the fog. The Owner selected the orange-red color.

Having just concluded my commission for the "US Federal Highway Administration's Blue-Ribbon Panel on Security of Tunnels and Bridges", not long after "9/11", defense against explosives was high in my mind when I conceptualized this bridge. I extended the solid concrete arm of the "Y" frame above the deck, thus making it much more resistant to an explosion on the deck.

The bridge looks better as a result. It also acts as protection against a possible truck collision.

The bridge is visible in fog

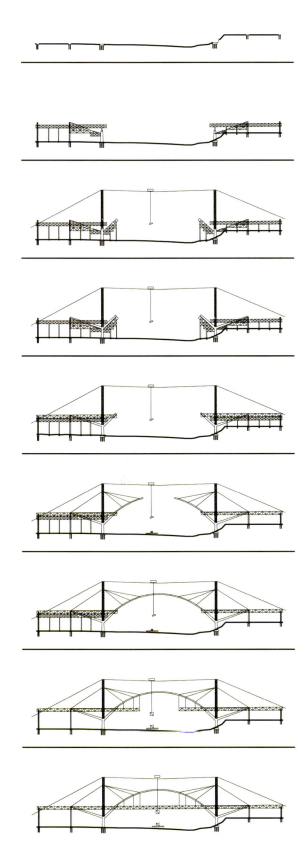

Construction scheme is a part of the bridge design process. One of the major considerations in construction is the supply of materials. Chongqing is a hilly city with narrow and winding streets. It is basically impossible to deliver construction materials and equipment through these streets in the City. Therefore, river transportation is the only logical means of delivery. But the large variation in water level in Chongqing's rivers is also a big problem for bridge construction. The normal high water level and the normal low water level of the Yangtze River at this site differ by about 23m. The highest high water can rise to 38m above the lowest low water level. Besides, during the low water season, only the southern portion of the river is navigable, which makes docking difficult.

To overcome this difficulty, I recommended a construction scheme using high lines. The contractor erected the world's heaviest high line with a capacity of 420 tons. After modifying the lifting procedure, the heaviest piece to be lifted was only 350 tons.

Construction began by building the prestressed concrete Y frame on local falsework. The arch ribs were erected using the high lines segmentally from both ends simultaneously and symmetrically. The arch ribs were held in place by a temporary stay-cable system. After completion of the arches, the truss girder was also erected using the high lines.

The construction with highlines went very well. It achieved a 3-day cycle.

The closure operation went very smoothly. It was important that the temporary stays be adjustable to correct any possible geometry deviation during erection. This way the closure operation was very simple.

Caiyuanba Bridge under construction

014 COMPOSING BRIDGES

Chongqing is a hilly city. The elevation difference between various levels of streets can be very significant. This makes the design of the alignment extremely complex.

In a hilly city like Chongqing, useable land is very precious. Transportation planning certainly cannot be the same as in a flatland city. It may happen that an entire hill must be removed just to accommodate an interchange. China is very mountainous. There are many hilly cities which are like Chongqing. Out of this necessity, our office led an effort to develop special design guidelines for transportation infrastructure design in hilly cities, which was published in 2007 by the Construction Department of the City.

Opening ceremony

Firecrackers are an indispensable part of a Chinese celebration

Caiyuanba Bridge at night

The Value of Aesthetics

An aesthetics purist once said: "Any art that also serves a practical purpose, it is no longer beautiful." A bridge engineer said: "Anything that does not serve a practical purpose does not belong to a bridge."

These are two extreme views about beauty. In my opinion, the underlying question is whether we believe beauty has any value. If beauty has value, it does not matter if an object serves any practical purpose; if beauty has value, making a bridge more beautiful should be part of the design.

As bridge engineers, we do not worry about what an aesthetics purist says. We believe any practical object can be beautiful, or ugly, no matter whether it is a car, a table, a house, or a bridge. Commercially, a merchant can fetch a higher price if the customer thinks it looks better; a beautiful house certainly is worth more than an ugly one. So, we do pay for beauty. If we pay for beauty, then beauty must have a value. Commercial builders have long understood this relationship. That is why they are willing to spend large sums of money to strive for the best architecture and landscaping so they can sell or rent buildings at a higher price. Manufacturers know that too. Even simple daily necessities like forks and spoons are well designed. A huge amount of effort is put into the styling of automobiles. Very often, the best-looking car becomes the best seller, not necessarily the best engineered one.

A beautiful environment makes people happy. We decorate our home so that we can feel more comfortable living in it. We travel to Grand Canyon, Guilin, and Yellowstone Park because the beauty there attracts us; we plant flowers in our garden because they look pretty. No doubt we have gotten used to having "beauty" as part of our life. And, we are willing to bear the cost for the enjoyment of it.

A bridge is a part of a city. No beautiful city can accommodate an ugly looking bridge. For example, a living room can be beautiful only if every piece of furniture in it is nice looking and blends well with each other.

If we agree that beauty does have value, we must then evaluate how much that beauty is worth! This question has been bothering decision makers and bridge engineers. This question can be very simply answered if we assume that a bridge in a city is just like a piece of furniture in a living room. The logic is the same! The core question is "affordability". We must understand what we can afford. If we are well off, we may buy a table at a higher price. If we are less well off, we may have to accept a plainer table. If we are really poor, we may have to make do with a makeshift table. In my experience, when buying a table was an unthinkable luxury, we made do by nailing a few boxes together from the fruit market. It served the purpose quite well. Would anyone do this now? I doubt that! It is not because it is not functional; it is because it does not look good.

This same logic applies to bridges. Today, we are not living in poverty so we can better afford to have beauty in our lives. Some people may still think that paying for aesthetics in bridges is a waste of money. Fortunately, for more important and visible bridges, most people do pay serious attention to aesthetics. They are willing to shoulder the cost of making the bridge more beautiful.

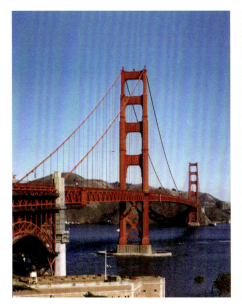
Golden Gate Bridge

The New San Francisco-Oakland Bay Bridge

The most striking example is the replacement of the Eastern Spans of the San Francisco-Oakland Bay Bridge in California, USA. The residents of the Bay Area did not like the bridge that the State Government was to build for them. They were willing to come up with 230 million US dollars to pay for the difference between a bridge they wanted and a bridge proposed by the State Government. They restarted the process of bridge scheme selection. In the end, they did choose the most expensive alternate. They believed, only such a bridge can match the beauty of the City.

This was the most expensive aesthetic decision among all the bridges I had ever been involved in. As Technical Director for the design of this bridge, I was deeply impressed by their decision. They organized a committee with 34 world experts to help them select the best-looking bridge scheme. The bridge they selected blends well with the surroundings and complements perfectly with the landmark Golden Gate Bridge and the Western Spans close by.

Someone may ask the question: "Is it really worth that much money?" From a different perspective, we may ask a question as reply: "If they had saved the $230 million to allow the construction of a less desirable bridge here and thus spoiled the beauty of the San Francisco Bay, would that be acceptable?"

Caiyuanba Bridge and Second Shibanpo Bridge

A Very Special World Record

On December 28, 2003, a groundbreaking ceremony was held for both the Caiyuanba Bridge and the new, Second Shibanpo Bridge, two world-record span bridges, on the same day, in the same city, on the same river, for the same owner. This, by itself, is certainly a historic event! It is really a great honor that I had the opportunity to oversee the design of both of these bridges.

Second Shibanpo Bridge · Chongqing

The new bridge is to the right side of the old bridge, a box girder bridge, with a main span of 330m, a world-record span for box girder bridges. The bridge was opened to traffic on September 26, 2006.

Chongqing is quite progressive in bridge construction. The First Shibanpo Bridge was built in 1981, with a span arrangement of 86.5m+4×138.0m+156.0m+174.0m+104.5m, connecting the central business district and the south district, or Nan'an, over the Yangtze River. Each span of that bridge has a 30-meter-long, drop-in girder at the midspan. At the time of its completion in 1981, it was one of the most advanced concrete bridge structures in China and the only major bridge over the Yangtze River in the City of Chongqing. The bridge was designed for an average daily traffic of 20,000 vehicles. By 2002, the volume of traffic had surpassed 80,000 vehicles per day. It was necessary to add new capacity to reduce the daily congestion.

The City requested a parallel structure adjacent to the existing bridge. This made it possible to use the existing approach ramp structures leading to and from the bridge without changes to the roads and interchanges in the vicinity.

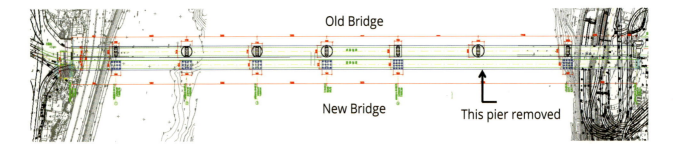

The new bridge is very close to the old one. The old bridge is a girder bridge; it would certainly look very awful should the new bridge be a cable-stayed bridge, an arch bridge or a suspension bridge. They just would not match!

For aesthetic reasons, the Owner requested that the new bridge be a box girder bridge like the existing bridge, and that all the piers must align with the piers of the existing structure. The Waterway Department, however, found that adding a pier adjacent to the existing pier between the two main spans would, in essence, create a "tunnel effect", which would render navigation hazardous at this location. Eliminating this pier would eliminate the tunnel effect but make the main span 330 meters long, which would be longer than all existing box girder bridge spans in the world.

Despite the risk of building a world-record span and higher costs, the Owner decided on a box girder bridge.

Traffic before opening of the new bridge

Such a box girder bridge can be built with concrete or steel. Currently, the world's longest steel box girder bridge span is the 300-meter span Ponte Costa e Silva in Brazil, built in 1974. A longer steel span has never been attempted. As the span gets longer, the thicknesses of the top and bottom plates become thicker. This significantly increases the difficulty of fabrication and cost. The bottom plate of a 330-meter span would be extremely thick. Fabrication would be very difficult, if not impossible.

The longest concrete box girder span is the 301m-span Stolmasundet Bridge in Norway. Norway has also built two concrete box girder bridges with spans close to 300m. These Norwegian bridges are all hybrid structures with a combination of normal-weight concrete and lightweight concrete. The lightweight concrete is used for the middle portion of the bridge to reduce weight. But the lightweight aggregate used for these bridges was imported from the U.S. This was not possible for the Shibanpo Bridge for reasons of time, schedule, and cost.

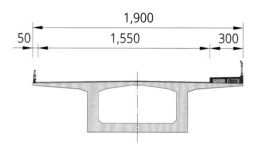 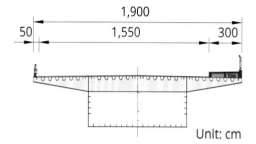

Unit: cm

In Chongqing, the low water season of the Yangtse River is from November to around May the next year. During this period, the water is low and a large portion of the riverbed is exposed so foundation work can be done without cofferdams. Therefore, it has distinct advantage to complete the foundations within one low water season.

The foundation of the Shibanpo Bridge has a total of 80 caissons with diameters of 2.00m and 2.50m. In order to meet the construction schedule, all caissons must be completed within one low water season. Here, the most expedient method of constructing these caissons was not by machine, but by manual labor. This is because all 80 caissons could be started simultaneously so only the one longest caisson was on the critical path. Certainly, this method can only be applied where labor cost is low and labor force is readily available. Chongqing offered both at that time.

Based on the Norwegian experience, it appears only logical that the New Shibanpo Bridge should also use something light for the middle portion of the main span to reduce shear and bending in the girder. We do have experience in lightweight concrete. During the design of the New Benicia-Martinez Bridge in California, we rigorously tested many commercially available lightweight aggregates in the U.S. These tests showed that only very few of them met all design requirements. Most of lightweight aggregates are low on modulus of elasticity. This probably explains why Norway had to import its lightweight aggregate from the U.S.

Currently, lightweight concrete is not popular in China. It is not economically feasible to import the aggregate from the U.S. It is also not feasible to carry out extensive testing to search for a suitable lightweight aggregate in China due to tight construction schedules. Moreover, with a span of 330m, the reduction in weight by using lightweight aggregate may not be enough. Hence, we decided to use a steel box for the middle 103m section instead.

The advantage of using a steel box section can be explained by a simple calculation. If we assume the superstructure is a prismatic girder with constant cross section and divide it into three sections of 110m each with self-weights of p_1 and p_2 as shown in the sketch, the fixed-end moment of the girder will be: $M_e = 4369p_1 + 4706p_2$.

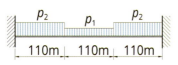

Assuming all three sections are normal-weight concrete, $p_1=p_2$, the bending moment at the fixed ends would be $M_e=9075p_2$. If we use lightweight concrete for the middle 110m, p_1 would be about $0.6p_2$, the fixed-end moment would be $M_e=7327p_2$, which results in a 20% reduction. If we use a steel box for the middle portion, the weight of a steel box girder is approximately 30% of the weight of a normal-weight concrete box girder, or $p_1 = 0.3p_2$, and the fixed-end moment of the girder will be reduced to $M_e=6017p_2$, which is only about 66% of the fixed-end moment of a full normal-weight concrete girder. A 34% reduction in bending moment has significant benefits in a long-span bridge of this dimension.

This bending moment of $6017p_2$ is equivalent to a full normal-weight concrete girder of 268m span. China has already built a 270m span concrete Humen Bridge. The technology and experience should be useful for this project.

There is a distinct advantage in using concrete for the pier portions and using steel for the middle portion in the girder. The bottom slab of the box girder near the main piers is rather thick and concrete is much easier to construct than steel.

Consider this: the allowable stress of a Q345 steel is 200MPa, the allowable stress of a C60 concrete is about 30MPa; thus, the capacity of a 2.00m thick concrete slab is equivalent to a 300mm thick steel plate. Undoubtedly, it is much easier to pour a 2.00m thick concrete slab than to fabricate and splice 300mm steel plates.

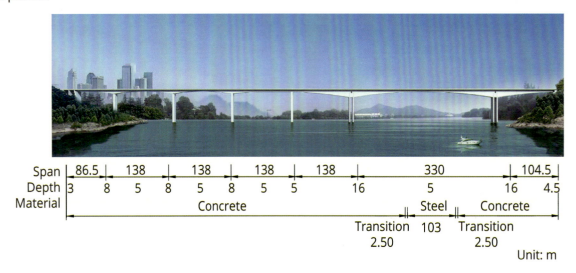

For the final design, the full steel box is 103m long. There is a 2.50m long composite transition segment at each end so the total length of the steel box is 108m long. The purpose of these transition segments is to transfer the forces in the concrete section to the steel section. It is like an overlapping splice. Post-tensioning tendons are used in these transition segments to assure a positive transfer.

Creep and shrinkage of concrete have been the topic of research for a long time. However, a precise calculation of their long-term effects on the deflection of a bridge girder is still approximate at best. For a 330m-long box girder, a small discrepancy may result in visible deflection. Therefore, a set of pre-stressing tendons are installed inside the steel box to compensate for any unanticipated deflection in the future, if this is necessary.

The concrete portions of the bridge were constructed by cast-in-place segmental method using form travelers. The steel portion could also be done in a similar way. However, this would require a different set of equipment and it would also take longer to build. In order to save time and cost, as well as to guarantee better quality, I decided to erect it as one big piece.

The steel box was fabricated in Wuchang, about 1,000km downstream from the bridge site on the Yangtze River. The 103m box was closed on both ends and was launched as a barge. It was towed from Wuchang to Chongqing along the Yangtze River. The steel box was properly designed for water and wave actions.

The steel box being towed upstream the Yangtze River

When the Owner decided to go ahead with the box girder bridge despite its being a world record, I was in Nanjing, meeting with the engineers of the Nanjing Second Yangtze River Bridge as a review consultant. Using fax and telephone, I communicated with engineers in Chongqing and within the evening, together, we established the final concept of the bridge: determining the length of the steel section, the girder depth, and the basic method of construction. We had the estimating group making a cost estimate of the new bridge for the Owner the next day.

The steel box section going through the lock of the Three Gorges Dam

The technology of lifting heavy loads using strand jacks has been quite well developed. The introduction of high precision electronic devices makes it more sophisticated, offering high precision and good maneuverability. All movements of the equipment shown in the picture are controlled by computers.

The total length of the steel box is 108m. It is divided into 3 sections: a 103m long middle section of regular steel box girder and one 2.50m long transition section at each end. The transition sections have double walls. After a transition section was lifted into place, the hollow space between the double walls was filled with concrete and prestressed against the concrete box.

The two transition sections are lighter. They were brought to the site on barges. The lifting of these two transition sections served well as a warm-up practice for the lifting of the 103m middle section.

Overheard on the street:

"These people, they could not even copy an old bridge correctly. How could they just forget a pier?"

While preparing for the lifting of the steel section, citizens were wondering why a pier was missing in the new bridge.

Second Shibanpo Bridge · Chongqing

Yangtze is a big river with rather swift currents. It is also a busy waterway. The Waterway Department allowed us to close the river for only 12 hours.

There were two major problems in lifting the steel box: how to turn the box 90 degrees while preventing it from hitting the existing bridge pier, and how to overcome the suction when lifting the girder out of the water.

Because the new bridge is so close to the existing bridge, there is not much room for error in maneuvering the steel box. To ensure the safety of operation, we used seven cables to stabilize the box. Each of these cables is anchored at the shore and can be adjusted to any length. This allowed us to turn the box and place it correctly at the desired location for lifting. The turning operation went well.

To overcome suction, we tilted the box on its leading edge against the water flow so that the vertical component of the current compensated the suction force when the box was lifted out of the water.

The entire lifting operation went very smoothly.

　　The steel box girder was raised to about 5m below its final position, the end covers were dismantled and the section was then raised to its final position. At its final position, the top and bottom flanges and the web plates were welded to the transition pieces at both ends. The stiffeners were spliced with bolts.

　　The Shibanpo Bridge was opened to traffic on September 25, 2006.

How Long a Box Girder Span Can We Build?

The success of the hybrid system in the Shibanpo Bridge inspires the question on how much longer we can extend the span length of a box girder bridge. Obviously, this is not purely an engineering question. With a longer span it may be more expensive than another type of bridge. There can come a time when we may not be willing to absorb the higher cost of a girder bridge over an arch, a cable-stayed or a suspension bridge.

When cost is not a criterion, the reliability of fabrication may become a limiting factor. The longer the girder span, the thicker the steel plates in the box will be. Theoretically, it is not impossible to weld or splice very thick plates, even in the field; the practicality, though, is a separate issue. Fortunately, with materials, equipment, and technology being continuously improved over time, these limitations may cease to be an issue; 30 years ago, we would have been hesitant to weld 50mm-thick plates in the field. That means, with continuing technological advances, what we presently think of as impracticable, or even impossible may become routine in the future. When that happens, "reasonable" span limits for bridges will be increased.

In 1967, in the design competition for the Neuenkamp Bridge over the Rhine in Duisburg, Germany, we won the two first prizes: one was a 350m span girder bridge using a new type of steel, NAXTRA70, which has a 700MPa yield strength. But because it was new and had never been used for a major bridge, the special precautionary procedures we specified made the fabrication and installation too expensive. The girder bridge was more than 30% more expensive than the world-record-span cable-stayed bridge scheme we also proposed. It was built and became the first fully welded long-span box girder bridge in the world. The cable-stayed bridge towers did use the new steel. But the towers of a cable-stayed bridge are mainly compression members, where the welding is less susceptible to fatigue problems.

This raises another issue in bridge building—quality control. When I designed the Neuenkamp Bridge in 1967, the German conglomerate I worked for, GHH, produced steel, had its own fabrication yard, performed the design and erected the bridge. Most importantly, we had our own workers and welders. They were permanent employees of the company, so we knew them well. We also designed and invested in their training. We could assign a specific worker to do a specific job because we knew he was good at it. This gave us confidence in using new materials and new technology because we could have control over their performance. Short of that, I might have designed the Neuenkamp Bridge differently!

Coming back to the question of how long a steel-concrete hybrid girder is technically feasible, the answer depends on many factors. The floating-in of the entire steel box girder like that of Shibanpo Bridge makes sense. It avoids most welding in the field. This makes use of thicker plates more acceptable. It may even be possible to eliminate field welding altogether by pouring the transition segment in place after lifting of the steel box. It would require a very rigid temporary bracing to restrict any relative movement between the steel section and the concrete sections. But this is not difficult. Or, we could splice the two ends with high strength bolts only.

Another controlling factor is the length of the steel section. There is a limit to how long it can be transported. The steel box of the Shibanpo Bridge is 103m long and weighs 1,400 tons. It is within the capacity of the lock at the Three Gorges Dam. A slightly longer section is still possible but requires more detailed maneuvering. If a much wider deck is required, it can be divided into two separate boxes. The weight of the segment is not a limiting factor with today's hydraulic lifting equipment. If the bridge is on an open sea where wave action is severe, the box girder must be designed for fatigue. The girder will be deeper for a longer span. This will require a deeper draft. Then the available water depth is another consideration.

Assuming all the above factors—cost, welding and water transportation—could be addressed successfully, my preliminary analysis showed that a 550m span with a 300m long steel box would be feasible. Obviously, each engineer could come up with a different answer because there are many assumptions made in such a study.

Dagu Bridge · Tianjin

The Dagu Bridge was opened to traffic on November 28, 2005

Dagu Bridge, Tianjin

Dagu Bridge

The Dagu Bridge is located at the center of the City of Tianjin, which is about 120km east of China's capital, Beijing. It is a part of the Downtown Redevelopment Project to revitalize the old City. As one of the first projects of the new Redevelopment, the City wanted the bridge to be a signature structure that could be a symbol of the City.

The bridge has a main span of 106 meters. It carries six lanes of traffic and two pedestrian paths, one on each side of the deck. The minimum width of each pedestrian path is 3.0m. Two of the traffic lanes are 3.75m wide and the other four are 3.50m wide. With a median divider, barriers, and railings, the minimum width of the deck is about 30m.

Aesthetics was the most important criteria for the design of this bridge. But the new bridge had to also satisfy several severe requirements and restrictions.

First, the bridge connects to local streets at both ends, so the elevation on both ends is fixed. The maximum allowable longitudinal slope of the deck is 3.5%. The river is navigated by cruise boats that require a certain vertical clearance. These boundary conditions, together, limited the maximum girder depth to only 1.3m near the midspan. Thus, the bridge girder had to be suspended from above, which meant an arch, a suspension, or a cable-stayed bridge. The bridge site is in a very high seismic zone and the top layer of soil there is rather soft so the foundation cannot resist high horizontal loads. That means the structural system had to be stable by itself. Consequently, only a tied arch bridge, self-anchored suspension bridge, or a cable-stayed bridge would work. It was decided that a cable-stayed bridge would not fit into this type of landscape.

In the preliminary design stage, three alternatives were proposed: two self-anchored suspension bridges and a tied arch bridge. All three alternatives would satisfy all design criteria. For a symbol of the City in the center of a major redevelopment area, the self-anchored suspension bridge, although very graceful, was not considered sufficiently visible due to its low profile. In addition, the City had already built a self-anchored suspension bridge and preferred a more exciting design.

All these factors resulted in the selection of the tied-arch bridge.

Outward leaning arches

Dagu Bridge · Tianjin

Conceptual design is the most important aspect of the design of a bridge. A proper conceptual design basically fixes the structural system, aesthetics, cost, and functionality of the bridge. It should also come with a construction method and solution of more important details.

Every bridge has certain restrictions. The conceptual design must properly consider and provide solutions for all these restrictions.

After we decided to design a tied-arch bridge, the chain of thought that led to the final configuration was as follows:

- *Due to the navigation requirement in the river, the arch must be above the deck.*
- *A regular arch bridge would have two arch ribs, one each side of the deck. They would have been over 32m apart.*
- *The girder is less than 1.4m deep which is not sufficient to span a 32m wide deck transversely, so I moved the two arches to the edges of the six traffic lanes. They are about 24m apart.*
- *If the two arch ribs are not connected to each other, they would have to be quite bulky in order to avoid lateral buckling. This is aesthetically not acceptable; two vertical arch ribs appear boring.*
- *It is customary to tie the two arch ribs together with struts to stabilize the arch ribs. This would look too messy here. It is aesthetically not acceptable.*
- *For the 106m span, a basket-handle configuration appears too flat.*
- *Instead, I design a three-dimensional structural system by having two planes of hangers for each arch rib. Thus, the ribs can be made very slender.*
- *Now, with two planes of hangers stabilizing each arch rib, I could tilt the arches any way I want. I tilt them outwards. This results in a very open view looking from the deck.*
- *The surrounding landscape is very asymmetrical so I increase the height of one arch to make the bridge more intriguing.*
- *The taller arch has a smaller inclination so that it does not lean too far outward; and*
- *This becomes the Dagu Bridge!*

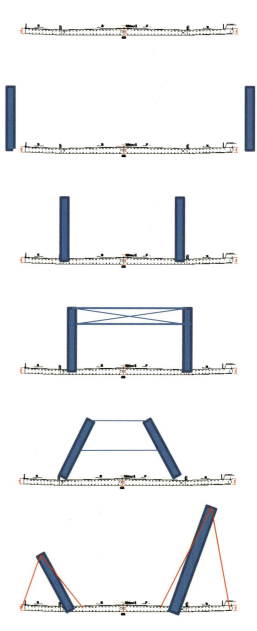

The pedestrian paths on both sides were expanded to provide a more spacious platform. The deck also has openings so that the pedestrians can see the water from the deck. Various shapes of the openings were studied and the upper one was selected for the final design.

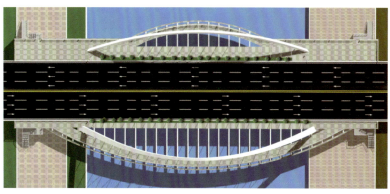

A variety of color combinations were studied. I preferred the white color for both the arches and the hangers.

The exposed cross-beams between the traffic deck and the pedestrian decks are painted dark grey to create a contrast. The pedestrian decks have a light grey color surface.

All hangers are stressed from the bottom so that the anchorages at the top are simple. Thus, the arch ribs appear very clean and elegant. All hangers are parallel wire strands with extruded HDPE jackets designed to the standard of regular stay cables.

From these pictures it is apparent that the trapezoidal arch rib looks much slenderer because the narrow bottom flange is more visible.

The final concept is a pair of asymmetrical, outward leaning steel arches. The ends of the arch ribs are all monolithically connected to the steel deck. A large transverse girder is placed under each end of the arch ribs.

The structure is a tied arch bridge. The steel bridge deck is large enough to serve as the tie. However, this would have introduced a large tensile force into the deck which might reduce its fatigue strength. Therefore, extra tie cables were used to introduce a compression force slightly larger than the horizontal component of the force in the individual arch rib. These ties are anchored at the transverse girders at the ends of the arch ribs.

The ties were designed to the same standard for regular stay cables to guarantee their durability and safety. They are made up of epoxy filled wire strands encased in high-density polyethylene pipes. The strands can be stressed and replaced individually, if required.

I used a steel box for the main girder for two reasons: the steel girder is much lighter which is good for this high seismic area, and, for a girder as shallow as less than 1.40m in depth, the box-shaped steel girder offers a higher torsional rigidity which is beneficial for such a structure.

The cross beams and the hangers are all spaced at 4.00m.

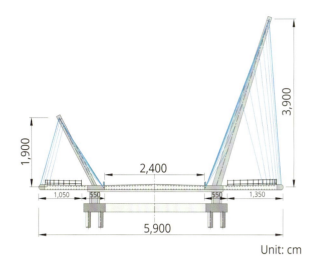

Unit: cm

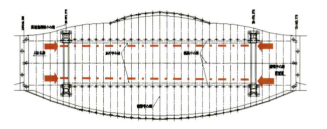

Above the bridge and in the vicinity

Every bridge has its special local conditions. The engineer must fully consider what the site offers and make use of the local advantages. There is no such thing as high tech or low tech in construction; the method that costs the least and can keep the schedule is the most suitable method of construction. The manual digging of the caissons in the Shibanpo Bridge described earlier is a good example of this idea.

At the time of construction, the river had only small fishing sampans, so local falsework was permitted. The deck was delivered in sections and welded together while resting on temporary piles. The arches were assembled on top of falsework supports resting on the finished deck. After the arches were complete, hangers were installed and stressed to a predetermined initial stress before the falsework was lowered. The hanger force at this moment needed only to be sufficient to keep the arches stable. These hanger forces were adjusted after the deck was lowered. This type of construction is straightforward and has very little chance of error.

Both arch ribs of the Dagu Bridge have trapezoidal cross sections. The small arch has a uniform section which is 1.30m high with 0.90m wide bottom flange and 1.30m wide top flange. The large arch has the same cross section as the small arch at its crown. Then the top flange width and the height both vary from 1.30m at the crown to 2.20m at both ends while the bottom flange remains a constant 0.90m wide.

People frequently ask why I did not use a round section. I have three reasons for using the trapezoidal cross section: first, because the large arch has a variable section, a trapezoidal cross-section is much easier to fabricate, especially for thick-walled sections; second, personally I feel the trapezoidal shape has much more character than the round shape; and third, since I decided to have all lights located at the deck level shinning upwards, the webs of a trapezoidal shape reflect the lights much better than a circular shape. A circular rib would always look half rounded no matter where the light comes from. Putting all light fixtures at the deck level is much easier to maintain and more economical as well.

The Haihe flows through the City of Tianjin like a golden dragon. Therefore, the entire Haihe Redevelopment is called by the locals "The Dance of the Golden Dragon".

The Dagu Bridge, with a large arch and a small arch symbolizing the Sun and the Moon, complements the Golden Dragon!

And the lights at the rim of the pedestrian deck? They look like stars!

"The Sun, the Moon, and the Stars"

A tranquil view of the bridge

I am very happy that I was able to design the Dagu Bridge according to all my own ideas. At the time of the conceptual design stage, I had already determined the shape and all major dimensions of the bridge, color of the paint, cable type as well as location and intensity of all traffic and aesthetic lighting. This is one of the rare occasions that no one interfered with my concept.

Whose Bridge is That?

Engineering is an art, not a science. The purpose of science is to search for truth, and the purpose of engineering is to create what is needed to satisfy human beings. Truth is unique. Creation is not unique. That is why an engineer can innovate and beautify what he creates.

Engineering is an art; sculpture is also an art. But there is a huge difference between them. A sculptor can spend a lifetime to perfect his sculpture, but an engineer must complete his product within specifications, time and budget. If an engineer neglects schedule and budget, he would cause big trouble to his client, or in most cases, the taxpayer. This can happen if an engineer works like a sculptor, treats his project as his own monument. The cost of material of a sculpture is relatively minor. The main cost of a sculpture is the time and effort being spent by the sculptor himself. If a sculptor strives to be perfect, the time and energy he spends is his own; it affects no one else. In bridge engineering, the amount of time and energy an engineer spends on the design is not significant, but the cost to strive for perfection could be enormous. This is no longer a question of his own choice.

More than 2,000 years ago, the great Roman architect, Marcus Vitruvius Pollio said: "Structures must be safe, functional and aesthetic." Today, we must expand this to "safe, functional, economical and aesthetic." Vitruvius worked for the emperor; economy was not a condition. We, the engineers of today, do not enjoy this luxury!

The basic function of a bridge is to satisfy the need of traffic. This is the basic reason why we build a bridge. I believe it is correct to place aesthetics behind economy. I am not saying that aesthetics is not important, but it must consider the purchasing power of a society. Obviously, the appropriate cost changes with time and location. In the case of the new San Francisco-Oakland Bay Bridge, the residents were willing to spend US$230 million to get a bridge they love. This shows most people are willing to pay for aesthetics. However, the engineer must understand what the people really want and not what the engineer wants. The bridge belongs to the people!

Today's China is much more well off than 30 years ago. People have a much better standard of living, cities are more beautiful, and people are more and more concerned about the environment they are in. Aesthetics of bridges has become a more important factor in the selection of bridge schemes—but budget is always important. Therefore, how to conceive the most beautiful bridge while still satisfying the requirements of safety, functionality and budget limits is the responsibility of the bridge engineer.

Second Wujiang Bridge · Fuling

The bridge was opened to traffic on September 25, 2009

Second Wujiang Bridge, Fuling

Fuling is a town 100 kilometers east of metropolitan Chongqing, located at the juncture of two rivers, the Wujiang and the Yangtze. The Second Wujiang Bridge is located close to the Yangtze River and is about 1.6 km downstream from the First Wujiang Bridge, which is a two-lane arch bridge completed in 1989. The First Wujiang Bridge is no longer capable of carrying today's heavy traffic. Therefore, a new crossing was necessary to meet the increasing traffic demand as the eastern portion of the town has rapidly developed.

The First Wujiang Bridge has a main span of 200 meters. However, a docking facility is located between the First and the Second Wujiang Bridges. After the Three Gorges Dam has been fully filled, the normal water level of the Wujiang River will be raised to about Elev. 175m. With this higher water level, it is anticipated that cruise ships may reach this portion of the river. Based on these circumstances, the Waterway Department determined that the main span for the Second Wujiang Bridge must be no less than 340 meters.

The bridge carries four lanes of city traffic and two pedestrian paths, one on each side of the roadway. The design flood level is based on a return period of 300 years, which results in a 180.75m high water level and a 135.80m low water level—a difference of almost 45m.

When we began the design for this bridge, the area around it had not been fully developed. However, we knew that this area was going to be very rapidly developed. In China nowadays, a city can be built within a few years' time. So, our design had to anticipate what would be coming in the next few years. And, sure enough, before we finished construction of the bridge, there were many buildings completed in the neighborhood.

This is China!

At the bridge site, the hills are very close to the bridge. Anticipating that many tall buildings would be erected soon after the bridge was built, the bridge should look as light as possible. I chose a single-plane, cable-stayed bridge as the best solution. It is light and it is more transparent than other bridge types. Accordingly, I have developed three single plane cable-stayed bridge schemes for this project.

The landscape is rather asymmetrical at this location of the river valley and a single tower, single-pole cable-stayed bridge would fit very well with the surroundings. But such a bridge has two drawbacks: first, the tower would be too tall for the area and there would be too many long cables; and second, the single-pole tower would be rather large because of its height and the bridge girder would have to be significantly widened to accommodate it and thus make the bridge more expensive. Consequently, I finally decided on a two-tower scheme.

For a cable-stayed bridge, the deck must always be widened to accommodate the cable anchorages. This widening is about 3 meters, no matter whether it is a single-plane cable arrangement or double-plane cable arrangement. A single pole tower must penetrate the deck in the middle of the deck, so the deck must be widened accordingly. If the bridge has a single cable plane and the tower stem is not larger than 3.00m, there will be no additional widening of the deck required. Obviously, single-pole towers are almost always larger than 3.00m at the deck level, so additional widening of the deck is necessary. Because the dead load of the girder in a long-span cable-stayed bridge usually dominates the weight of the deck, the cost of the deck is closely proportional to the width of the deck. Consequently, reducing the width of the single-pole tower at the vicinity of the deck is important.

The tower of a cable-stayed bridge is supported by the cables in the longitudinal direction of the bridge, so the stiffness in that direction

is less important. In the transverse direction, however, the column of a single-pole tower acts more like a cantilever, so it requires a certain stiffness to remain stable under the loads from the cables. In order to limit the widening of the deck to a minimum, it is important to search for a tower shape that provides the required stiffness with the smallest width. In this respect, a rectangular shape is more effective than a circular shape. Besides, a rectangular column can be stretched longer to get a larger cross sectional area without increasing the width. That was the reason why I chose the rectangular column over the round column, even though the round column probably looks slightly better. This is a compromise between aesthetics and economy!

The design of the Second Wujiang Bridge has three basic requirements: it must be aesthetically pleasing; it must be economical; and the piers must be sufficiently strong to resist the potential impact from barges.

The town of Fuling is rather hilly. There are steep slopes on both sides of the Wujiang River with very little flat land. High levees are constructed along both banks of the river to keep out high water, so as to maximize useable land.

The Waterway Department required that the bridge provide a minimum vertical navigation clearance of 10 meters measured from the highest high water level; the elevation of the bridge is high above the land on both banks. This results in very steep ramps on both ends of the bridge and very short end spans.

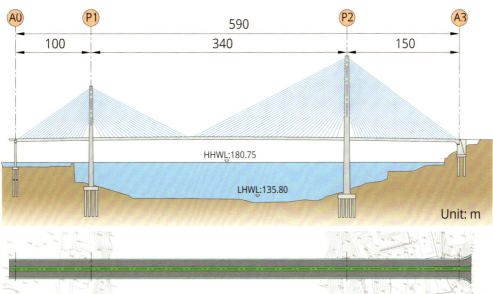

We compared various bridge types: arch, suspension, and cable-stayed bridge for this site. An arch would have been too imposing. A suspension bridge would have been too expensive and it could have an anchorage problem. A single-plane cable-stayed bridge is more graceful and fits the landscape very well.

The landscape is not symmetrical on the two sides of the bridge and the hills are very close to the bridge. The northern end span is only 100m long and the southern end span is 150m. For a 340m main span, a 100m end span is only 29.4% of the main span. That is too short. But the local condition does not allow a better arrangement. In fact, on the south bank, the topography is so restricted that a three-level spiral ramp is needed to bring the traffic from the bridge down to the local streets.

For this rather asymmetrical situation, my solution is an asymmetrical cable-stayed bridge with two towers of different heights. The tower height above the deck is proportional to the length of the end spans. Thus, the total length of the two side spans is 250m, about 74% of the main span. It is a more appropriate proportion.

The ground line is also not symmetrical. Hence, the lower portions of the towers are 63m and 73m above the top of the pile cap for the south and the north towers, respectively. These portions of the towers have a variable box-shape cross section, increasing in size from the top to the bottom. The tower shafts above the deck also have a box-shape cross section, tapering from the deck to the top. One tower is 105.4m above the deck and the other tower is 66.4m above the deck.

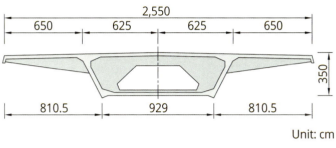

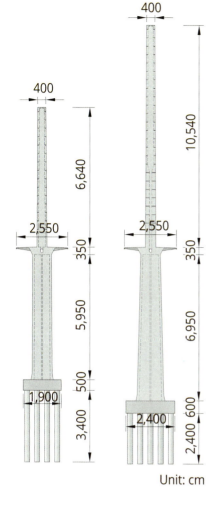

Typical cross-section

The single-box cross section with a single plane of cables is an efficient arrangement. It can be constructed by means of form-travelers like a concrete girder bridge. This is a popular construction method in China.

The cables are anchored at the center of the box girder to a vertical diaphragm. Two prestressing tendons are placed inside the vertical diaphragm and wrap around the stay-cable anchorage to carry the vertical component of the cable force to the bottom of each web. The horizontal component is transferred directly to the top slab of the box girder through the anchor block.

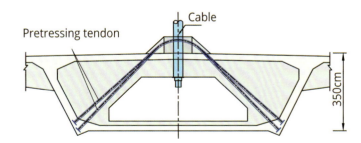
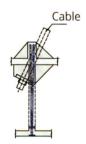

The single-cable plane in conjunction with a single-box girder arrangement of the Second Wujiang Bridge is very similar to the Second Crossing of the Panama Canal. The Second Panama Canal Bridge was opened to traffic in 2005. It has a main span of 420m and a deck width of 34.30m, both of which are larger than those of the Second Wujiang Bridge. The concept is the same except that in the Second Panama Canal Bridge, I used a triangular steel frame to transfer the vertical component of the cable force from the anchorage point at deck level to the bottom of the webs, while here, I used a pair of prestressing tendons embedded in a partial concrete diaphragm instead. The reason is that in Panama, labor is more expensive, so a prefabricated steel frame saved time and was more economical, while in today's China, labor is less expensive so a concrete frame with posttensioning was more economical.

The circular ramp

Designing bridges in China can be challenging due to limitations in space. In total land area, China is about the same as the United States. But, most of China is mountainous. The flat or useable land in China is less than half of that in the U.S. In addition, China's population of 1.35 billion is 4.5 times that of the U.S. As a result, cities are sprawling along narrow river valleys between steep hills. To make things worse, the rivers in these towns often flood with very high water levels. Any bridge crossing the rivers in these towns must be built high above the riverbanks. Fuling is one such town.

The elevation of the bridge deck is 210m. On the northern end, the local streets are at about the same level as the bridge deck. They carry traffic to the riverside drive underneath. However, on the southern end, the local streets are on the riverbank at an elevation of 175m. The difference in elevation is 35m. There is little land on the southern end that can accommodate a long ramp structure. As a result, a three-level circular ramp is used to carry traffic from the bridge down to the local streets.

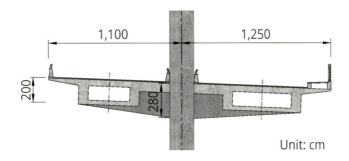

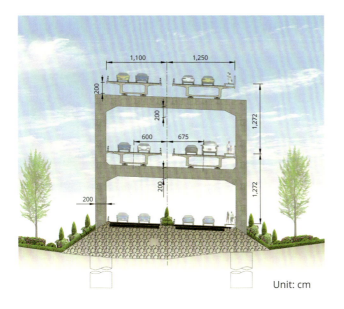
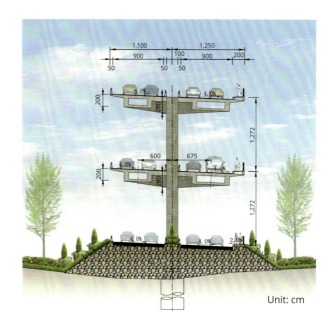

There are two ways to support a spiral ramp: using a portal frame with double columns or a series of single columns at the middle between the two ramp structures. The radius of this ramp is very small, so the double-column solution would appear messy. Therefore, I decided to use a single row of columns in the middle. For such an arrangement, the ramp girders must have torsional rigidity, so box girders were chosen. The columns are spaced at about 20 to 25m apart. The columns are 2.00m by 3.00m wide. The radius of the centerline of the ramp is 45m.

Each column supports several levels of the girder. The completed structure looks very graceful.

Single-column support

At the time when the Second Wujiang Bridge was under construction, the Three Gorges Dam had not been filled to its final water level, so the water level in the low water season at this site was still rather low. The foundation was built without a cofferdam during the low water season. Once the substructure was completed up to an elevation above the high water level, the construction could continue without interruption.

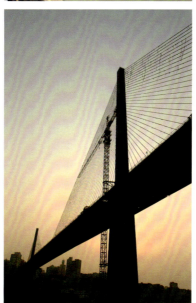

Second Wujiang Bridge · Fuling

Sanhao Bridge · Shenyang, Liaoning

The Lily on the Hwun River

Shenyang is the capital of Liaoning Province and is one of the largest cities in that Province. The City's economy was originally built on heavy industries. However, in an effort to improve the area's living environment, almost all of Shenyang's factories were moved out of the City in the last two decades. Today, the area features new developments, modern shopping malls, and residential neighborhoods. The Hwun River runs through Shenyang. The water level is usually low, except during flood seasons. The City is planning to construct a small dam downstream to elevate the water level so that the river will have a constant water depth year-round. This will make the river navigable for cruises and pleasure boats. High-priced residential buildings have sprung up on both banks of the river, creating a need for bridges.

The Sanhao Bridge is the ninth bridge crossing the Hwun River. It connects the two parts of the City. It is 2.5km downstream from the existing Qingnian Bridge and 3.8km upstream from the Gongnong Bridge, both continuous girder bridges. Both banks of the river near the bridge have been made into river parks with beautiful landscaping and river walks. The vicinity of this bridge will feature high-end residential complexes so the City requested that aesthetics be a priority in selecting bridge alternatives. In other words, the bridge had to be a signature structure!

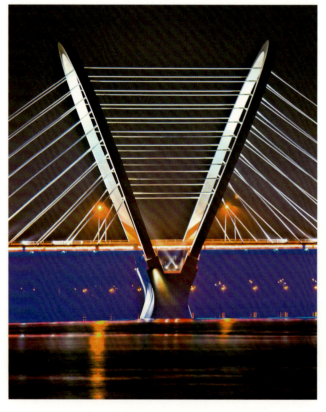

Sanhao Bridge, Shenyang, Liaoning

The Sanhao Bridge carries six traffic lanes and one 4.50m-wide pedestrian/bicycle path on each side, resulting in a total width of 32m without cable anchorages and 34m with cable anchorages. The total project is 1,430m long; the bridge portion is 900m long. The main span arrangement is 35m + 100m + 100m + 35m = 270m.

The elevation is determined by the streets on both ends. With the future navigation requirement, the girder can only be 2.40m deep with a 100m span.

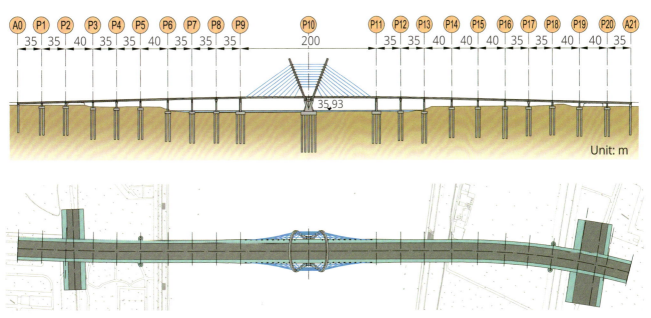

The bridge is designed for Chinese City Class A loadings. The design speed is 50km/h, the design flood is based on a return period of 300 years, and the seismic design is based on seismic intensity 7 (Chinese Code) with a ground acceleration of 0.10g. The maximum longitudinal slope is 2.50%.

The Sanhao Bridge is the first bridge designed based on the new concept of the "partially cable-supported girder bridge". This design concept achieves economic efficiency by fully utilizing the capacity of both the girder and the cable supporting system. [M C Tang, *Rethinking Bridge Design—A New Concept*, Civil Engineering Magazine, Vol.77, July 2007, USA].

There are three ways to provide partial cable supports in a partially cable-supported girder bridge. They can be called "partially cable-stayed girder bridge", "partially suspension cable-supported girder bridge" or " partially arch supported girder bridge", depending on whether the girder is supported by a set of stay cables, suspended from a suspension main cable, or hung up by an arch. This concept is best applied to short- to medium-span bridges where the girder depth is restricted but the girder can still contribute a healthy amount of capacity to carry a large portion of loads acting on it. This design concept is especially suitable for bridges in China where many smaller towns are located between two mountain ranges with a medium size river running across the middle of the town. The bridges crossing these rivers have a construction depth restriction because the bridge deck elevation is controlled by the elevation of the local streets on both riverbanks, while at the same time, river transport is still important for the local economy, so that the spans cannot be too small.

For the Sanhao Bridge, this design concept allows the use of a concrete main girder instead of a steel girder. Currently in China, a concrete girder is much heavier but significantly less expensive. Unlike a traditional cable-stayed bridge where the tower carries almost the entire load of the girder, the tower of this bridge carries only about half of the load.

An arch is better suited to carry in-plane loads than out-of-plane loads. Therefore, the forces in the horizontal cables that tie the two inclined tower ribs together are properly adjusted so that there is no out-of-plane force acting on the tower ribs under permanent load conditions.

An arch is not an efficient form for a tower that must carry vertical loads. The vertical component of the cable forces creates a bending moment in the arch rib. It is important to reduce the vertical component of the cable forces. In a regular cable-stayed bridge, the top cables are usually the biggest cables. But in the case of a partially cable-supported girder bridge, this is not so.

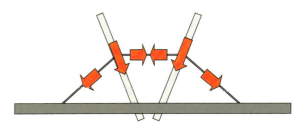

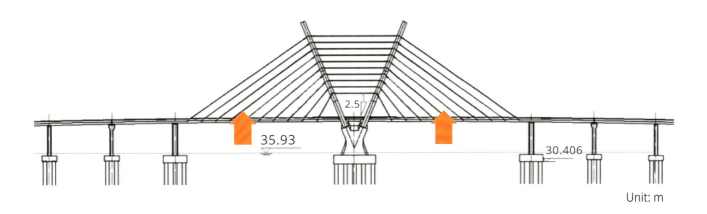

Unit: m

For a partially cable-supported girder bridge, the girder provides sufficient stiffness to satisfy the deformation requirements. Thus, the function of the cables and towers is mainly to create a set of uplift forces to balance the loads on the girder. For this purpose, the middle cables, not the top cables, are most effective because they create an uplift force at the midspan. So, the forces in the top cables can be reduced to a minimum. Consequently, the bending moment in the arch-shaped tower ribs can be drastically reduced.

In fact, the cable forces in a partially cable-supported girder bridge can be assigned rather freely. If the group, as a whole, can produce a bending moment in the girder that is sufficiently large to supplement the missing capacity of the girder, the structure works.

Sanhao Bridge · Shenyang, Liaoning

At the time of construction, the river was not yet navigable. Taking advantage of this, the bridge girder was built on falsework.

A multi-cell, box cross-section was selected for the bridge girder for two reasons: aesthetics and torsional rigidity.

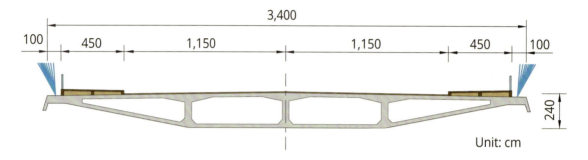

The arch ribs were assembled and welded together on the bridge deck

072   COMPOSING BRIDGES

The tower ribs were assembled on top of the completed bridge deck

The bridge girder was built on falsework. After the girder was completed, the tower ribs were delivered to the site in segments. They were welded together on top of the bridge deck in a flat position. A temporary tower frame was installed between the two ribs to rotate them into their final position, using strand jacks. The lifting operation took approximately 11 hours.

Sanhao Bridge · Shenyang, Liaoning

Vertical rotation

After the tower leaves were raised to their final position, the horizontal cables were installed to their exact length. After several horizontal cables were installed and stressed, the tower ribs were able to stand up by themselves.

The inclined cables were then installed and stressed, two pairs at a time, symmetrical to both bridge axes.

Most work platforms were attached to the arch ribs before they were fully raised.
All cables are made up of epoxy filled seven-wire strands encased in a high-density polyethylene pipe.

Each cable anchorage point has a work platform

The bridge looks different from different viewpoints: from afar, it looks like a huge lily floating on the river. From up close, you are surrounded by cables spanning in all different directions and the bridge feels very high-tech, spectacular, and empowering!

Opening ceremony of the bridge held on October 10, 2008

Jiayue Bridge · Yuelai, Chongqing

A view on the Jiayue Bridge

The Jiayue Bridge crosses the Jialing River near the town of Yuelai, Chongqing. The surrounding area will be developed into a high-end residential neighborhood. Therefore, the Owner desired to build a beautiful bridge to attract potential home buyers.

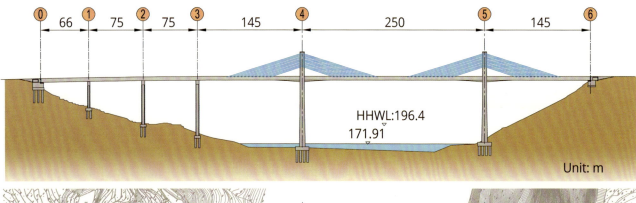

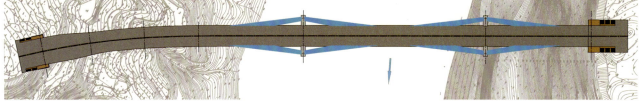

For such a landscape, a traditional cable-stayed bridge was not ideal because the towers would have been too tall and it would have had too many cables that would look quite distracting. Hence, I decided on a partially cable-supported girder bridge that has shorter towers. However, the towers could not be too low as to render them inefficient.

The river traffic here consists mainly of barges and fishing boats. The required main span was 250m. However, the bridge has a total length of 756m.

The Jialing River runs through a deep valley at this location. The bridge is almost 90m above the river. The deck elevation, however, is close to the top of the hills on both riverbanks.

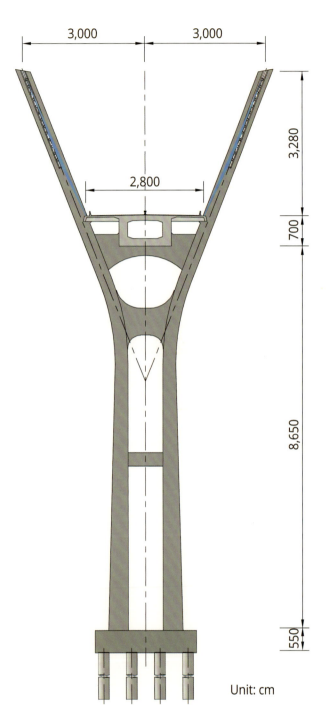

The success of the Dagu Bridge convinced me that inclining the tower arms outward gives people a much more pleasant view from the bridge deck. With today's construction technology, the premium to pay for this inclination is relatively minor.

During construction, the pair of tower arms was connected with a temporary horizontal cable to balance the outward bending due to the additional load of the formwork.

The correct bridge type name of the Jiayue Bridge is partially cable-stayed girder bridge, a type of partially cable-supported girder bridge.

The Jiayue Bridge is not an "extradosed bridge" even though it looks like one. The difference lies in the height of the towers above the deck.

The word "extrados" denotes the external face of an arch. This word was introduced to bridges to mean a girder bridge with longitudinal prestressing tendons extended above the top deck in the vicinity of the pier to increase their effective eccentricity from the center of gravity of the girder. Hence, extradosed bridge towers must be sufficiently low so the cables carry almost no live load and thus, can be designed as external tendons with higher allowable stresses. The Jiayue Bridge towers are taller and the cables are designed as stay-cables.

The design of the towers must consider the possibility of ship impact at various water levels. During the high-water season, possibility of ship collision increases. For this purpose, concrete towers are more suitable.

In order to match the tower shape, the approach piers all have a similar shape with double columns.

The main girder has a single box cross section in prestressed concrete. Form travelers are used to construct the girder. Cables are epoxy filled seven wire strands in an HDPE pipe. The strands in the cable can be individually adjusted and replaced if necessary. The towers are reinforced concrete. The cables are anchored in a steel box inside the concrete tower column.

Chongqing is called one of the three "ovens" of China, indicating how hot it can be. Temperatures can hover above 40°C for prolonged periods during the summer and it is rather rainy in the winter. To offer pedestrians refuge from the sun and rain, I placed the pedestrian paths underneath the wing slabs of the upper deck. This also resulted in a narrower bridge deck, which is structurally more efficient.

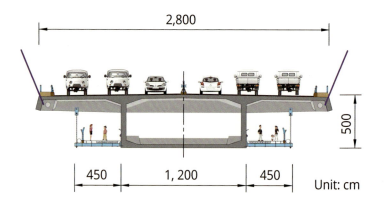

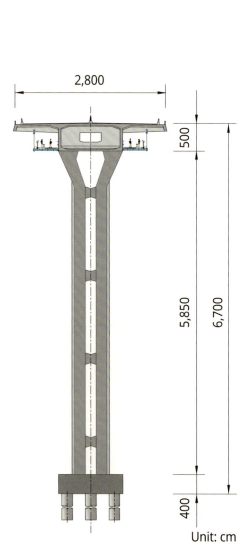

Approach pier

Putting the pedestrian paths under the deck may cause pedestrians to feel boxed in because the walkway is right next to a wall. Such a pedestrian path must be sufficiently wide to offer more openness to pedestrians.

The walkways are suspended from the cross beams of the deck on the outside and are attached to the web wall on the inside. The walkway deck is made of steel to reduce the overall weight.

For security reasons, we did not provide any crosswalk between the two walkways for the entire length of the bridge. However, there is a wide-open space underneath each end where people can walk from one side to the other side. There is also room for other facilities, if necessary.

The walkway deck is covered with a colored mat for a more soothing feeling underfoot. The walls can be used for art exhibitions during special occasions.

Here comes the concrete

Here comes the anchorage box

Horizontal ties stabilize the arms

Tower construction

Jiayue Bridge · Yuelai, Chongqing

Working day and night

The spacious walkway

The landscape of the Jialing River Valley is gorgeous!

Taking a walk on the Jiayue Bridge walkways across the Jialing River is a popular pastime for the members of the neighborhood. From here, one can see a long stretch of the Jialing River Valley, on both sides of the bridge.

Night view of the bridge before the aesthetic lighting is installed

A view from the lower valley (the bridge was opened to traffic on Febuary 11, 2011)

Jiayue Bridge · Yuelai, Chongqing

Yuyun Bridge · Yingkou, Liaoning

The Yuyun Bridge is part of the main thoroughfare on the central axis of Yingkou, a town in the southeastern region of Liaoning Province

Yuyun Bridge · Yingkou, Liaoning

The Yuyun Bridge is a small but very delicate structure. It is very visible from the parks along both banks of the river, which are very popular promenades used by citizens. Aesthetics was a priority in the design.

The span length of the bridge is 13.5m + 46.6m + 13.5m. The width of the bridge is 37.0m at the middle span and 43.3m at both side spans.

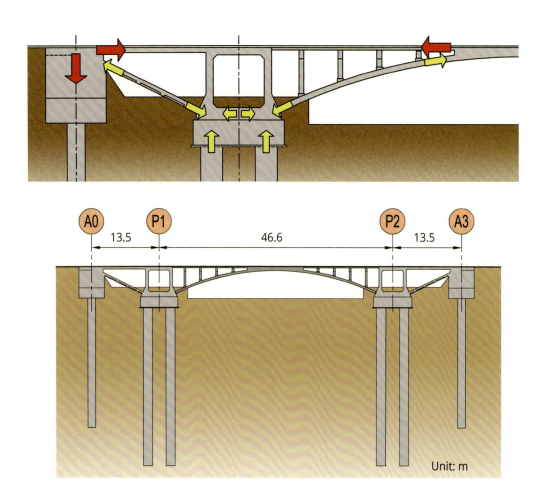

The challenge in the design of this bridge was to solve all technical problems and create a beautiful bridge within a very low budget.

The site does not have many restrictions. Labor cost is also low. It is very suitable for building a concrete arch bridge.

To make it special, we decorated it in a Rococo style.

The deck is very close to the water surface. Therefore, the arch is very flat. It has a span-to-rise ratio of 9.5. This resulted in a pair of high horizontal thrusts at each abutment. The soil is very soft and unable to resist such high horizontal forces. Using piles to resist these large horizontal forces would have been expensive. Placing a tie in the river was deemed unsafe. The opening for a pedestrian walkway at each abutment made the problem worse.

This problem was solved by adding end spans to the bridge: with a counterweight and a strut at each end of the end spans, we easily balanced this pair of horizontal forces. This way, the bridge only transfers vertical load to the foundation, which can be carried by long vertical piles to better soil layers down below.

The design can be named an "extended tied arch bridge". If we take away the pedestrian walkway/bicycle paths crossing underneath the deck at each end of the bridge, the structure is akin to a tied-deck arch. In a tied arch, there is no need to transfer any horizontal force to the piers.

The river is actually a man-made canal dug from dry land. The bridge was built before the canal. Taking advantage of that, the contractor dug out a portion of the soil and placed small falsework on it to build the bridge. The dirt was removed after the bridge was completed.

The arch rib is a 45cm thick solid plate. The deck plate is 20cm thick, supported by vertical struts spaced at 3.20m on center.

The pedestrian tunnels at both ends of the arch are about 4m wide and 4m tall.

The bridge is supported by a total of sixty 1.50m-diameter concrete piles. Twenty piles under each main pier are 50m long and the others, under the ballasts at the end of the bridge, are 25m long.

The bridge architecture is in the Rococo style. Rococo is an European architectural style popular during the 18th century at the end of the Baroque Era. It was very popular for palaces and churches. It is very colorful, lively and exciting. It represents the royal architecture of the kings and emperors of that time.

The railing along the river is a typical style of Chinese architecture. This kind of railing can be found in most palaces and temples in China, both in color and in style. It is also the architecture of the emperors.

Here, the two royal styles blend exceptionally well with each other. Strolling along the promenade next to the river is a very pleasant pastime.

This is a merging of two royal styles. What a royal treatment!

On the Yuyun Bridge

Tuojiang First Bridge · Luzhou, Sichuan

Twin structures, span: 90m + 135m + 90m
Prestressed concrete girder bridge
Opened to traffic on February 9, 2010

Tuojiang First Bridge · Luzhou, Sichuan

Unit: cm

Luzhou is a hilly city at the junction of the Tuojiang and Yangtze Rivers. The existing First Tuojiang Bridge is an arch bridge with seven spans of 45 meters. It was built in 1965. It is a narrow, two-lane bridge with a pedestrian path on each side. The total deck is 14m wide. The traffic has long outpaced the capacity of the bridge, so additional capacity is needed.

The new bridge had to provide four traffic lanes with a horizontal navigation clearance of 80m. But citizens are comfortable with the old bridge and they also wish to keep the old bridge for sentimental reasons even though it no longer satisfies current navigation regulations.

The old bridge

One of our schemes was to build a pair of wider new bridges and use the old bridge as a pedestrian mall. The space between the two new superstructures can be filled with skylights.

Since the river traffic is currently not busy, and the existing spans of 45m can still meet the actual needs of river traffic of today, the old bridge can be used for a certain period of time. Yet, the new bridge had to be built to current standards with an 80m-wide navigation clearance and it had to be taller as well.

There was no space for a new bridge to be built alongside the old bridge, if it had stayed in its current location. There would have been too much demolition on both riverbanks. The connections to local traffic would have been difficult as well.

In this hilly city, newer developments have been moving toward higher elevations, so most new traffic comes from local streets at higher levels. Therefore, we chose to put the new bridge higher and connect it to the streets on the higher levels. The superstructures of the new bridge were built adjacent to the existing bridge, one on each side, but with some overlaps so as to avoid demolition of the buildings near the ends of the bridge. The two superstructures each carry two city traffic lanes plus a pedestrian path and they are 10m wide each.

To achieve aesthetic compatibility with the existing bridge, the piers of the new bridge were aligned with the existing bridge piers. Thus, the new span length had to be a multiple of 45m, which is the length of each span of the existing bridge. The new bridge also had to provide a horizontal navigation clearance of 80m. This resulted in a 135m main span and two 90m side spans.

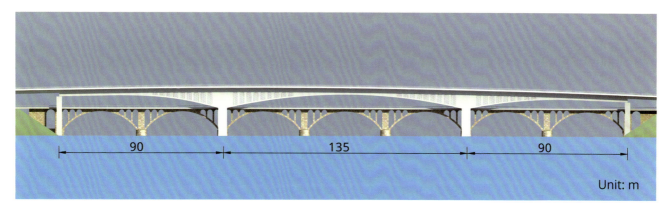

Each of the two new superstructures is a cast-in-place, prestressed concrete box girder constructed with form travelers. To assure the safety of the people on the existing bridge (which must remain open during construction of the new bridge), a sliding cover was placed on the existing bridge deck. This cover moved along with and was located right underneath the form travelers, so that the deck of the existing bridge was shielded from falling debris from the travelers.

The new bridge foundations were supported by 2.5m-diameter caissons. Special care was taken to avoid possible damage to the existing piers.

Construction of the bridge took 23 months.

Taijiang Bridge · Sanming, Fujian

The City of Sanming is built on both banks along the Sha River between two mountain ranges. The Sha River is a very narrow river and runs through the middle of the City. The City has already built seven bridges over the river. These bridges are of a rather conventional design. The Taijiang Bridge is the eighth bridge and will probably be the last bridge to be built for some time. The citizens desired to have a signature structure that would serve as a symbol of the City.

Considering that the areas on both ends of the bridge were to be developed into a recreational and modern business district, an aesthetically pleasing bridge was essential. It had to be an exciting bridge that people would stop to look at and enjoy.

We submitted two bridge schemes, both of which were cable-stayed bridges. The Owner selected the one with an arch shaped tower.

108 COMPOSING BRIDGES

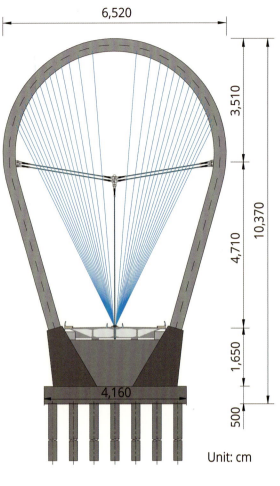

An arch-shaped tower is not the most efficient structural shape for a bridge tower. Structural efficiency translates into economy. The most efficient structural system is the most economical solution for a bridge. But, when aesthetics is a major requirement for a design, the goal then becomes to not only design the most efficient structural shape, or the least expensive solution, but also to create a concept that addresses both aesthetics and structural efficiency. The design of the Taijiang Bridge is one such case.

"Acceptable in structural efficiency" can be directly defined as "within budget" in this case. The Owner gave us a budget and asked for the most beautiful bridge for the price. This is our solution!

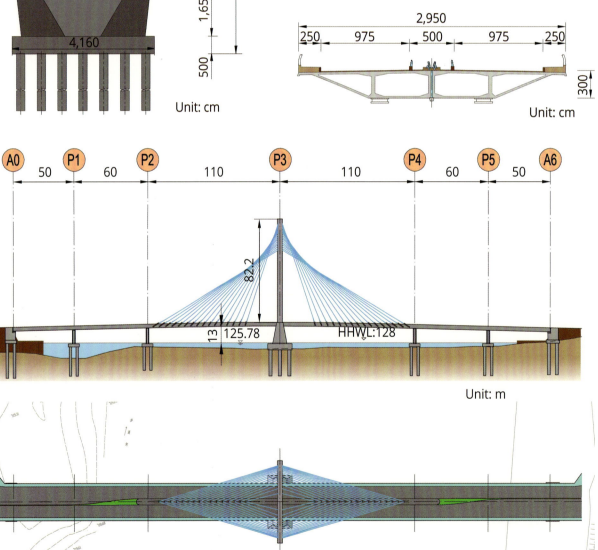

110   COMPOSING BRIDGES

A conventional, straight vertical tower certainly does not qualify as a signature bridge for this location. To make it look more intriguing, the Taijiang Bridge has an arch-shaped tower with an inverted cable arrangement. Neither of these two choices appeared to represent an efficient structural system to carry vertical loads. But it does work quite well. The rationale is as follows:

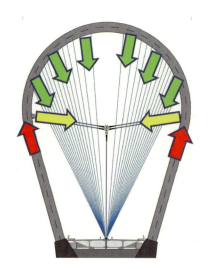

The tower is comprised of three parts: the arch, two inclined struts, and a horizontal tie cable.

People understood the efficiency of arches way before the Romans. But it was the Roman Empire that built many spectacular arch bridges. An arch is a good structural system to carry vertical loads. However, for an arch under vertical loads to work, there must be a strong abutment at each end to resist the large horizontal thrust there. Otherwise, the arch functions as a beam that has a very high bending moment.

A tied arch solves that problem by balancing the horizontal forces through the force in the tie. That is why we have placed two horizontal cables at the bottom of the arch to serve as ties. The upper portion of the Taijiang Bridge tower is basically a tied arch. If the hanger forces are all equal and radial to the arch, there would be no bending moment in the arch rib. But, since they must be anchored to the deck, the hangers in this case are not radial and the arch rib has a bending moment. Still, its magnitude is manageable.

The lower portion of the tower consists of two outward-leaning struts. They carry the vertical loads from the arch to the foundation. The outward inclination of these struts creates another pair of horizontal forces. The horizontal tie cable takes care of this pair of horizontal forces as well.

The bridge is symmetrical in both the transverse and longitudinal directions. Therefore, we can adjust the forces in the cables to eliminate all out of plane forces in the arch rib. Because all cables are anchored at the longitudinal axis or center line of the bridge deck, the arch will not experience any transverse load no matter what load is acting on the bridge deck. Certainly, there will be eccentric loading on the deck, but the eccentricity will be taken up by the torsional moment of the deck.

The force in the horizontal tie cables is very high, and the cable anchorages are large. These large anchorages cannot be placed inside the arch rib. So, they are anchored to the inner face of the arch. They cannot be stressed nor adjusted. Nevertheless, cable force adjustment is important to assure the proper internal forces in the arch. To address this, I installed a vertical tie cable, with its upper end connected to the middle point of the horizontal tie cables and the lower end anchored to the bottom of the concrete girder. In this way, by adjusting the vertical tie force we can control the forces in the horizontal ties.

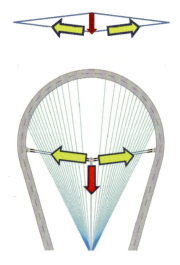

The force in this vertical tie cable was adjusted from the bottom of the deck. When the force in the vertical tie-cable is known, we can calculate the horizontal tie-force. This is because the forces at the joint must be in equilibrium all the time. From a structural analysis standpoint, the relation is nonlinear. But, in lieu of a tedious nonlinear analysis, the simplest way is to determine the geometry of these cables and calculate the force in the horizontal cables based on equilibrium.

Erection of the keystone segment

Taking advantage of the fact that the river is not yet navigable, local falsework was used to construct the bridge girder. This is the most convenient method of construction. The arch was erected after the girder was complete.

Fujiang First Bridge · Hechuan, Chongqing

The Fujiang First Bridge is located in downtown Hechuan, Chongqing. It carries two city traffic lanes and two pedestrian/bicycle paths. But it is wide enough to be expanded to four traffic lanes in the future.

The bridge was opened to traffic on December 31, 2010.

The original Fujiang Bridge

The original Fujiang Bridge was a double-curvature arch bridge. This type of arch bridge was popular in China 30 years ago because it is very efficient and economical. Each arch rib itself has a shell-like cross section that provides higher stability. Therefore, its cross-sectional area is minimal. It was an excellent solution for medium-span bridges at a time when China was poor and building materials were scarce. The original bridge was too narrow and required too much maintenance so the City decided to replace it.

For the replacement, we offered three alternative schemes. Scheme #1 was an arch/girder combination that has a classic appearance and a larger navigational clearance. Scheme #2 was a cable-stayed girder bridge with the same span arrangement as in Scheme #1. Scheme #3 was a girder bridge, the most economical solution that reuses the piers and foundations of the existing bridge.

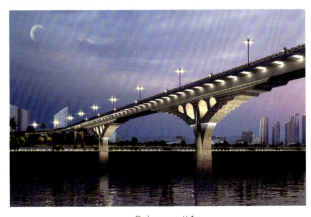
Scheme #1

Schemes #2 and #3

Since the water level at this location will rise after flooding of the Three Gorges Dam downstream to its final level, more river traffic requiring larger navigational clearance can be expected in the future. A larger horizontal clearance is preferable. Hence, the City selected Scheme #1 for final construction.

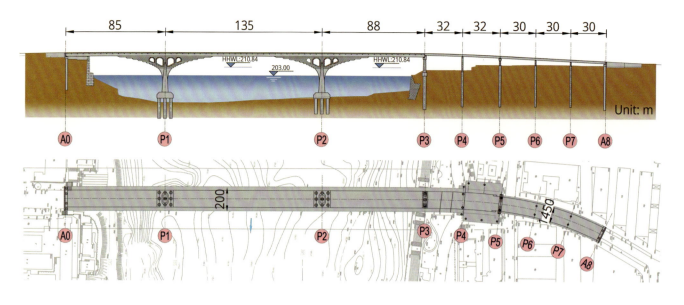

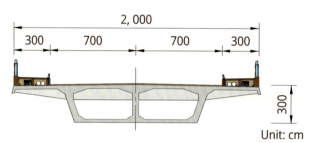

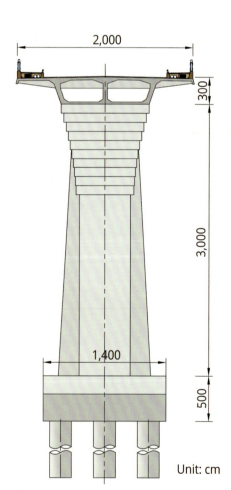

The new Fujiang First Bridge in Hechuan was to replace an existing bridge and be built at the same location. The original bridge was an old arch bridge, which was found to be deficient and had to be replaced. The original bridge was the first bridge built in the City and served as the only bridge for a long time. It had made its share of contributions to the economic development of the City, so the citizens were quite sentimental about it.

The original bridge was a deck arch with small spans. The new bridge required longer spans due to increased navigation on the river. The citizens hoped that the new bridge would be similar to the old bridge but building a long-span arch bridge at this location would have been too expensive, especially since the completion of a dam downstream raised the water to a much higher level. On the other hand, the higher and steadier water level significantly improved the landscape of the City and navigation.

To satisfy the wishes of the citizens, we conceptualized a bridge that is a combination of a partial deck arch and a partial girder. It has a classical shape that is quite unusual. It was built as a cantilever bridge with form travelers so the cost was reasonable. On December 31, 2010, the bridge was opened to traffic with tens of thousands of enthusiastic citizens at the scene. There were lots and lots of happy faces!

The New Fujiang First Bridge in Hechuan, Chongqing

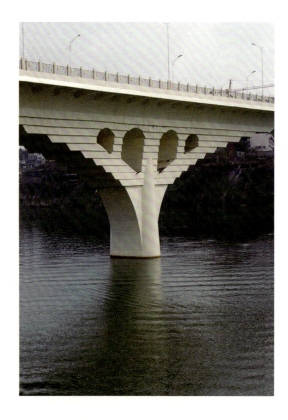

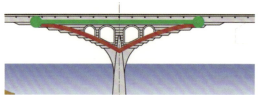

The new Fujiang First Bridge has a 135m-long main span flanked by two side spans of 85m and 88m. Its structural system is a combination of deck arches and girders. The portion above each of the main piers acts like a deck arch with a tie at the top. The deck, however, is a box girder that runs over the entire bridge length. Simply put, it can be called a continuous box girder resting on two tied-arches.

The girder is 3m deep. As a rule of thumb, a 3m-deep box girder should be able to span about 60 meters. In our case, the girder length between the two arches is less than 50 meters.

If we took out the girder portion of the bridge it would be a typical deck type tied-arch, as shown in the sketch. An arch usually does not have bending moment, only axial force, at the crown. What we have done here is to take the two halves of the arch apart and fill in the gap with a box girder.

The box girder is designed as a prestressed concrete segmental bridge. It was built using form travelers. This is a well-tested method in China since its adoption in the early 1970s.

The footings are supported by piles.

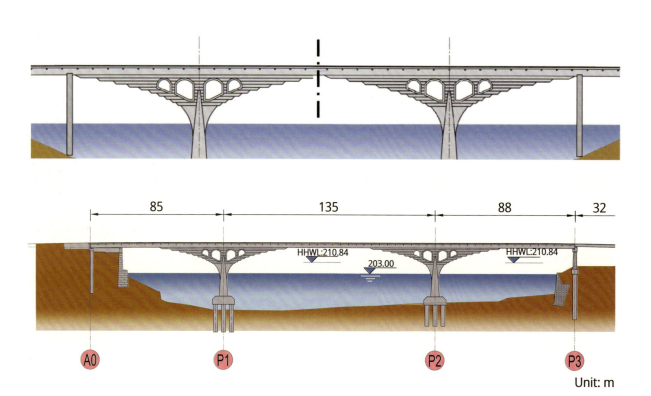

Unit: m

120 COMPOSING BRIDGES

The pier table, a short section of the girder on top of each main pier, was constructed first using local falsework. This section must be long enough to accommodate the two form travelers to be erected on top of it. After the two travelers are erected, subsequent segments can be cast using these form travelers.

Construction of the first few segments was a little more complicated because of the openings in the girder itself. For this stage of construction, the structure acts like a Vierendeel truss until the completion of the entire arch. The verticals of the Vierendeel truss, however, are rather robust, so it can be built efficiently without additional strengthening.

The overlapping shape of the web wall does require special attention. It is more labor intensive. Fortunately, labor costs in China are not high; thus, this type of construction is feasible.

Fujiang First Bridge · Hechuan, Chongqing

World Records

"We shall not waste money chasing after a world record; but we shall not be afraid of creating a world record if required."

People love records, especially world records. Athletes spend their lives preparing for the Olympics, hoping to be the fastest runner or the highest jumper in the world. A gold medal is a glory for life!

It is understandable that people are also excited about designing and building the longest span bridge in the world—this is merely another attempt at making a world record.

But there are differences between a bridge world record and an Olympian world record: the cost and the consequence.

First, the world record is the only goal and purpose of the athlete. There is no other purpose for his efforts. The basic reason why we build a bridge is to carry traffic. A world record is never the primary reason for any bridge. Therefore, paying additional cost to achieve a world record is beyond any reason why we would build the bridge.

Second, when an athlete dedicates his or her life to train for the Olympics, it comes at a cost of his or her time and life. Whether the value of a medal is worth the cost is a personal decision, and it is separated from society's values as a whole. But when someone builds a world record bridge, he or she is not spending his or her own money, but, rather, the taxpayers' money. He or she should not have the luxury of making that decision based on personal ambitions.

Third, if an athlete fails, and most of them must fail because there is only one record holder in the entire world, the consequence is not significant to society. But if a bridge could not be completed, the consequence to society would be significant.

Fourth, there is a limit to what an athlete can achieve. The human body is not a machine that can be designed. Up to a certain point, no matter how hard one trains or how much money one spends, a world record may simply be beyond reach. A bridge span record, however, is merely a question of funding. My estimate shows that with the current technology, we should be able to build significantly longer span bridges, be it a girder bridge, a cable-stayed bridge, an arch bridge or a suspension bridge. Hence, building a longer, world record span does not require much hard training or research—just money. When the span gets close to the current world record, the cost of the bridge increases exponentially with the increase in span length. If the world record is not a representation of any advancement in technology or innovation, why should we spend a large sum of money for this rather worthless matter?

Certainly, if the site requires a world record span, we shall not be afraid to build it.

Bridges Under Construction

At the time of publication of the Chinese Edition, the following bridges were under construction.

Nanping Bridge · Hechuan, Chongqing

Both the Fujiang First Bridge and the Nanping Bridge are in the City of Hechuan. The Fujiang First Bridge crosses the Fu River and the Nanping Bridge crosses the Jialing River. Construction for these two bridges began at the same time. The Nanping Bridge is longer and therefore takes longer to build.

On one end of the Nanping bridge is one of the most well-known historic monuments of China, Diaoyucheng. People desire to have a nice-looking bridge to welcome the numerous tourists coming here every year.

The bridge site is similar to most bridge sites along the Jialing River, graceful and poetic. For such a landscape, neither an arch bridge nor a regular cable-stayed bridge would be appropriate. Therefore, we proposed two bridge schemes, both of which were cable-supported girder bridges. The shorter towers of an cable-suported girder bridge fit better in this more tranquil landscape.

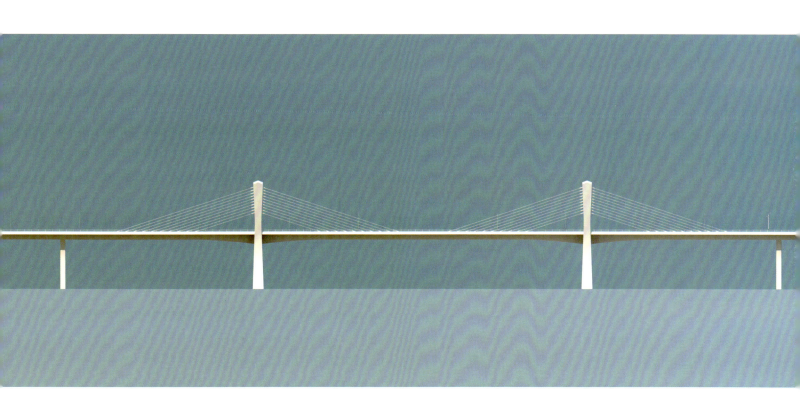

Nanping Bridge · Hechuan, Chongqing

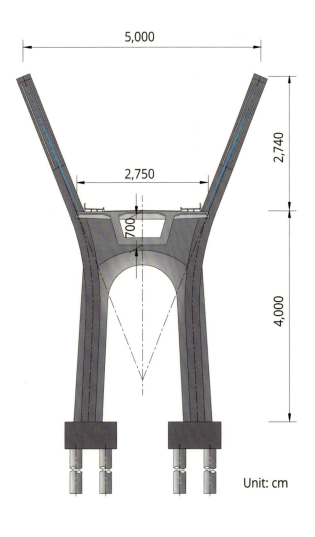

The main span of 190m was based on the requirements established by the Chongqing Waterway Department. The deck is 27.5m wide, with four lanes of city traffic and a pedestrian/bicycle path on each side. It is a prestressed concrete single-cell box girder with transverse ribs supporting a concrete deck slab.

The girder is monolithically connected to the towers. This simplifies the construction of the pier tables and the subsequent segments because local support is not necessary once the pier table is poured.

The cables are designed according to the requirements of regular stay cables.

The towers have a hollow box cross section. Post-tensioning was applied to transfer the girder reaction to the tower diaphragm and further to the tower legs.

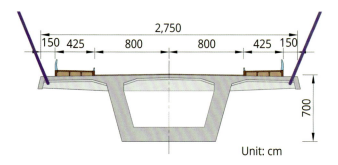

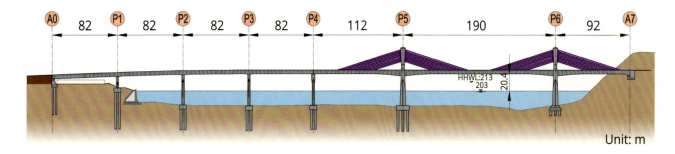

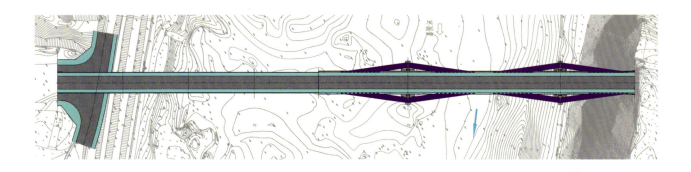

126   COMPOSING BRIDGES

The Nanping Bridge crosses the Jialing River in Hechuan, connecting the downtown area with Diaoyucheng (in Chinese, Diaoyucheng means "*Fishing City*"), a historic ancient army depot well known for its heroic resistance against an overpowering Mongolian army.

Some historians say the Battle at Diaoyucheng changed the history of the world. Here is how the story goes:

In 1258, the Mongolian Great Khan, Mongke, a grandson of Genghis Khan, personally directed the battle with 40,000 troops to try to overrun Diaoyucheng, a not so large rock island in the Jialing River. But, for about a year, he failed to conquer the island. Instead, he was wounded and died in August of 1259. His brother, Hugelu, who was preparing to invade Egypt and Syria at that time, stopped the campaign in Europe and returned to China to fight for succession and try to become the Great Khan against his brother Kublai. He lost. As a result, the Mongolian Empire broke up into several factions and did not advance much further, in Europe nor elsewhere.

A few historic footnotes: Mongke's death in Diaoyucheng made him the only Great Khan ever to die in a battle; indirectly, that pivotal event halted the unstoppable Mongolian military advancement in Europe; and Diaoyucheng became the only City to have been able to successfully resist a Mongolian invasion. The City fought off the Mongolians for 20 more years, until 1279, when the island signed an amicable treaty to become part of the Yuan Dynasty, which was established by Kublai in China.

Diaoyucheng is now a favorite tourist attraction.

The Nanping Bridge is supported by large-diameter piles. The lower portion of the substructure was built during the low water season to avoid needing large cofferdams.

The girder was built by the segmental cantilever method using form travelers after the towers were completed. This method is a well-established construction method in China.

The single box is 4.5m deep, except in the vicinity of the towers where it varies up to 7m. This type of cross-section is very suitable for segmental cantilever construction.

The bridge was opened to traffic in 2011.

The Nanping Bridge in Hechuan, Chongqing
A cast-in-place segmental prestressed concrete bridge

Twin River Bridges · Chongqing

130 COMPOSING BRIDGES

With a population of 32 million, Chongqing is one of the largest cities in the world. The metropolitan area of Chongqing is divided by two rivers, the Jialing and the Yangtze, into three regions. In recent years, several bridges have been built to facilitate traffic through these three regions of the City. Despite these efforts to relieve congestion, the rapid growth of the City continues to outpace transportation planners' traffic projections and the existing bridges are not sufficient to handle the ever-increasing traffic. In response to this problem, the City's plan is to build approximately 800 km of light rail to reduce pressure on the city roads. The Twin River Bridges are part of that light rail system.

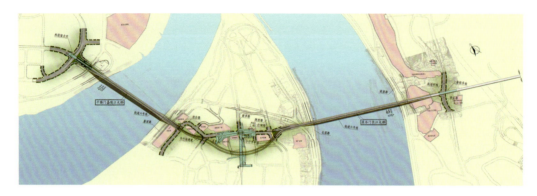

The two bridges are located at the tip of the Yuzhong Peninsula, connecting the central business district with both the newly developed Jiangbei business district in the north and the recreation quarter on the south bank of the Yangtze River. The new Dongshuimen Bridge crosses the Yangtze River and the new Qiansimen Bridge crosses the Jialing River; together, they are called the Twin River Bridges. A tunnel in Yuzhong District connects these two bridges, allowing both light rail and road traffic from the southern district to flow though Yuzhong to the northern district without interruption. Both bridges have four lanes of city traffic as well as pedestrian paths on their upper deck and two light rail tracks on their lower deck. Because of the bridges' high visibility, aesthetics was an important consideration during the bridge type selection process.

The configuration of the Dongshuimen and Qiansimen Bridges had to satisfy aesthetic, geographic, and technical criteria. Since they are located between three city districts, they had to be harmonious with three disparate surroundings. They had to complement one another, and they had to stand on their own. Finally, the bridges could not obstruct views of the City from various vantage points.

Navigational requirements and local geology demanded main span lengths of 445m and 340m for the Dongshuimen and Qiansimen Bridges respectively. The lack of a side span at the Yuzhong side of the Qiansimen Bridge limited the number of towers to only one.

In addition, the bridge girder had to be at least 13m deep to accommodate the light rail on its lower deck. Similar to the Caiyuanba Bridge, I made the girder into a truss for two reasons: to offer transit passengers a more open view of the area and to increase the transparency of the bridges themselves. The City had just constructed two major arch bridges in the area, the Caiyuanba Bridge and the Chaotianmen Bridge. Therefore, an arch bridge was not a favorable choice.

We preferred to not have a conventional cable-stayed bridge because it would obstruct the view of the City. The tower of a 340m span, single-tower cable-stayed bridge would have protruded approximately 170m above the deck level. The bridge is roughly 60m above normal water level so the total height of such a tower would have been approximately 230m tall—taller than almost every building in the City. A conventional cable-stayed bridge would have had too many cables, further hindering the view of the City. A regular girder bridge would not have been suitable either because the spans are too long.

Consequently, the choice was between a partially cable-stayed girder bridge or a suspension bridge for their relatively shorter towers and fewer cables. Both minimalist designs disturbed the surrounding space the least.

Keeping in mind the location of the bridges in relation to the Yuzhong Peninsula, it was natural that the two bridges should be similar. Therefore, we conceptualized two schemes for these two bridges—a pair of suspension bridges and a pair of partially cable-stayed girder bridges.

The Suspension Bridge Scheme

The suspension bridge scheme was comprised of a pair of single-tower suspension bridges, each with a 496m main span. The side spans of both bridges were 250m long. They both had two planes of cables. The towers are 100m above the deck.

In the Yuzhong Peninsula, where the rock formation is very fractured, it would have been difficult to anchor the main cables in the ground, unless an extremely huge anchor block and a major tie back system were used to transfer the cable force deep into the ground. Because there were numerous buildings in the area, the tie-back anchors would have compromised the foundations of these buildings. Therefore, conventional suspension bridges were not suitable for these two bridges.

A self-anchored suspension bridge scheme was also studied. A 496m span, self-anchored suspension bridge was technically possible, despite its record-setting length. However, it would have been very expensive because the girder would have to be erected first on temporary falsework before the cables were installed. The busy river traffic and swift current during the high water season posed a danger due to possible ship collisions. Consequently, the idea of two self-anchored suspension bridges was discarded.

To resolve this problem of the anchorage, a special concept was conceived.

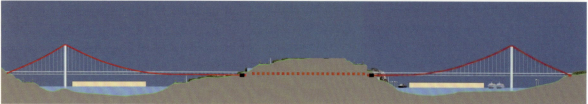

Dongshuimen Bridge · Tunnel · Qiansimen Bridge

The transit tunnel that connects the two bridges runs under a street on the Yuzhong Peninsula. The tunnel is about 600m long. Instead of anchoring the cables individually to a foundation in the ground, we extended the main cables of the two suspension bridges over the length of the tunnel and connected them to one another, so that the cable forces of the two bridges would equalize each other. However, because the two cable forces would not be equal all the time, we built two anchor blocks, one at each end of the tunnel. These two anchor blocks were tied together by two large connection cables, slightly larger than the two suspension cables. They were stressed against one another to a force slightly higher than the maximum cable force of the suspension bridge cables. The suspension bridge cables were then anchored to these anchor blocks. In this way, the anchor blocks always exert a compression force on the rock formation, which is preferable. The connecting cables run through a separate chamber underneath the transit tunnel. The chamber was excavated and constructed simultaneously with the transit tunnel. Because this cable chamber was directly underneath the transit tunnel, right-of-way issues did not exist and the cost was minimal. The force in the connection cables is basically constant, and a higher working stress is allowed.

Aesthetically, the pair of suspension bridges was attractive and compatible with one another. Additionally, they complemented the landscape and were very transparent in elevation.

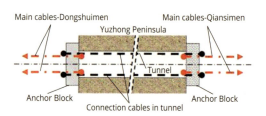

Connection of main cables of the two suspension bridges through the tunnel

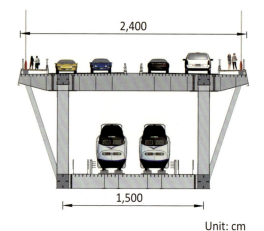

Cross section of suspension bridge truss

Partially Cable-Supported Girder Bridge

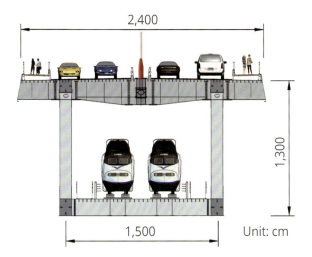

The partially cable-stayed girder bridge scheme was selected for the final design.

Compared to the tower of a suspension bridge, the tower of a conventional cable-stayed bridge is typically twice as tall. In this scenario, while the span of the bridge may be reduced to 340m, its tower would still remain 170m above the deck. Such a tall tower would not complement the surrounding landscape. Furthermore, a conventional cable-stayed bridge would have had too many cables that obstruct views of the city. Therefore, a pair of partially cable-stayed girder bridges was selected.

The concept of a partially cable-stayed girder bridge was applied successfully to the design of several medium-span bridges in China, such as the Sanhao Bridge in Shenyang and the Jiayue Bridge in Chongqing. While the spans of the Twin River Bridges are much longer, the girder depths of these two bridges, at 13m, are also much deeper. Thus, the span to girder depth ratio is comparable to that of the previously designed medium-span, partially cable-supported girder bridges.

The minimum main span length of the Dongshuimen Bridge is 445m. Thus, the span to girder depth ratio is 445/13 = 34.2. The minimum main span length of the Qiansimen Bridge is 340m. Its span to girder depth ratio is 312/13 = 24.0. These ratios are within the range of partially cable-stayed girder bridges.

The Dongshuimen Bridge has two towers while the Qiansimen Bridge has one tower. All three towers are similar, each about 100m high above the upper deck. Each tower of the Dongshuimen Bridge carries 9 pairs of cables. The tower of the Qiansimen Bridge has 11 pairs of cables. All the cables form a single plane on the center line of the bridge.

The truss of both bridges is 13m deep by 15m wide. The depth includes room for an inspection wagon underneath the cross beams. The 15m width accommodates some curvature of the tracks inside the bridge length. The truss is torsionally very rigid, which allows the use of a single plane of cables in the middle. The light rail has very tight restrictions on the allowable deformation of the structure. However, the girder is very stiff and has no problem meeting these requirements.

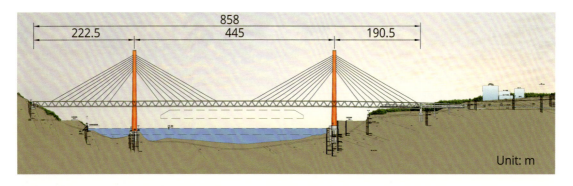
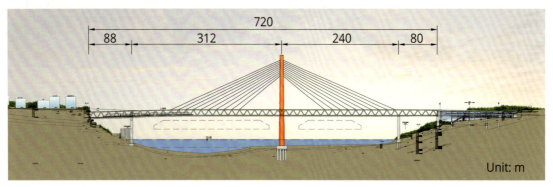

The upper deck is an orthotropic steel deck with a minimum deck plate thickness of 16mm with flat ribs. The main floor beams are between 2.00m to 2.70m deep. Other regular floor beams are 1.20m deep. The lower deck consists of four longitudinal beams located directly under the rails. The lower floor system is also an orthotropic deck with open ribs. The orthotropic deck serves as a platform next to the tracks. It acts monolithically with the lower chord of the main truss.

Orthotropic steel bridge deck has been widely used for long span bridges since its introduction in the early 1950s. However, cracks have been observed in several bridges. Most problems can be traced to the quality of the welds. In recent years, most engineers prefer trapezoidal ribs. Trapezoidal ribs are more efficient than open ribs. But a trapezoidal rib can only be welded from the exterior side of the rib to the deck plate. This weld requires very high-quality control which, unfortunately, is not always available. So, for the Twin River Bridges, I decided to use open flat ribs. The welds of flat ribs to the deck plate is significantly simpler because the open ribs can be welded from both sides of the rib and this kind of weld is very common in steel structures. Open ribs, especially flat ribs, are less efficient. They weigh more. However, for these two bridges, this is not a disadvantage because the additional cross-sectional area can be fully utilized as a part of the top flange of the girder.

Experience, from as early as the 1960s, has shown that bridges with thin deck plates can cause problems in both the steel deck and the pavement. During the design consultation of the Nanjing Second Yangtze River Bridge in China, I recommended that the deck plate to be at least 14mm. Most bridges in China built after the Nanjing Bridge had changed to 14mm or thicker and these bridges have been performing quite well. Considering that overloaded trucks are very common in China nowadays, I believe 14mm may still not be sufficient. Hence, I used a minimum thickness of 16mm for the Twin River Bridges.

Designing the bridge based on the concept of a partially cable-stayed girder bridge gives us freedom in choosing the cable forces. In these two bridges, we have fixed the maximum cable force under the worst load condition to be 1,400 tons each. This results in all cables having the same size.

The cables are made up of bundles of individually epoxy filled and sheathed seven wire strands. Each of these strands can be replaced individually, if necessary.

The configuration of the towers is very Chinese. It looks like the shuttle of an ancient Chinese weaving machine.

I have always wanted to design a tower more distinctly Chinese. For over a year we worked to develop and to perfect such a tower shape. The Twin River Bridges offers the first and best opportunity of its application. This tower shape is very delicate. It must be sufficiently tall and must have good proportionality in length between the upper, or the above deck portion, and the lower, the below deck portion. It cannot accommodate a wide bridge girder—that would look too bulky. Most new bridges in China have six lanes. They are too wide for this tower shape. The condition of the Twin River Bridges is just perfect for its application.

When we select a curvy configuration for a concrete structure, we must pay attention to the contour of the concrete surface. Form work is a relatively expensive item in concrete construction. Making the form reusable for many lifts is a good way to achieve economy. The external contour of the Twin River Bridge towers is circular with the same radius constant from top to bottom, except that it is narrower at the top and wider at the bottom. The top portion of the tower is almost straight.

The upper ends of the cables are anchored at the open space at the top of the tower between the two vertical halves. Here, the two halves are connected by two large concrete blocks, one each at the top and at the bottom of the open space. These blocks have a rounded top surface covered with a thick steel plate so they can be used to support temporary cables during construction and for future maintenance, if needed. The anchorage boxes also serve as additional connections of the two halves. Furthermore, transverse post-tensioning tendons inside steel pipes are used to stress these two halves together so that the entire tower head acts like a deep beam, but with spacious openings to let sunlight through.

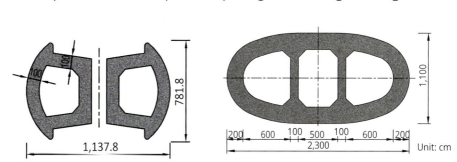

Cross section at top and bottom of tower

There is a tie beam at the kink, located at the juncture between the top and the bottom portions of the tower to take care of the horizontal force created by the change of slope of the tower arms.

The bottom, solid portions of the towers are extended higher so the variation in water level will not affect the appearance of the towers. This also provides better protection against possible ship collision.

Twin River Bridges · Chongqing

Color selection: we studied many different color schemes and combinations

138   COMPOSING BRIDGES

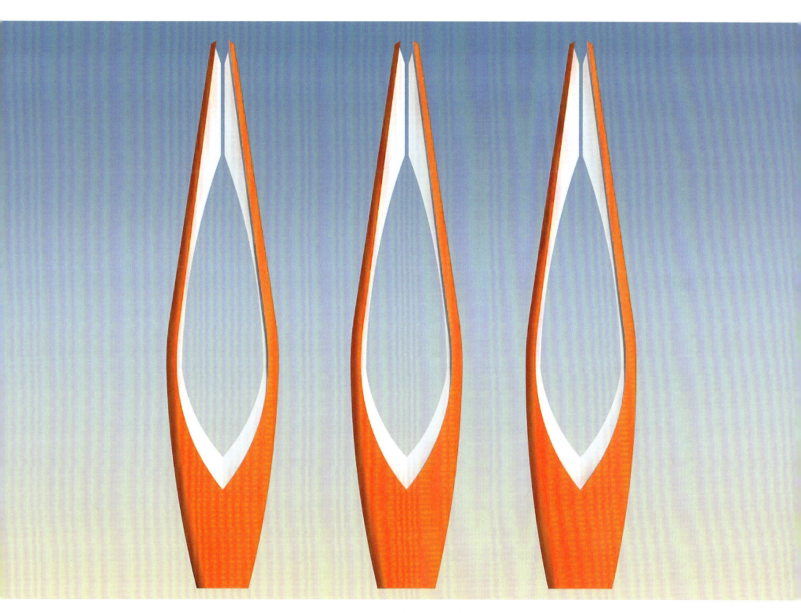

Fine-tuning of the tower shape

Twin River Bridges · Chongqing

The Dongshuimen Bridge (over the Yangtze River) was opened to traffic on March 31, 2014.

The Qiansimen Bridge (over the Jialing River) was opened to traffic on April 29, 2015.

View from the bridge deck

Innovation

Innovation is one of the most talked about subjects in China nowadays. The government has also set up many awards to encourage people to innovate.

Innovation is very important. Whether a country becomes a strong country or can win a competition all depends on its ability to innovate. But what is innovation? I once defined it thusly: "to create value by a new approach". For example, a successful bridge must satisfy four basic requirements: "safety, functionality, economy and aesthetics." Each has its own value: the value of safety, value of functionality, value of economy and value of aesthetics. A new method that can increase the sum of these four values can be recognized as innovation. Certainly, the evaluation of these values can be rather subjective—it may vary with time, location and people—but in general, certain consensus is possible.

I once suggested that the path to innovation is to find answers to three basic questions: "Why?", "Why not?" and "What if?". The first question "Why?" is to challenge the status quo; the second question "Why not?" offers an opportunity for your new idea; the third question "What if?" is to remind yourself to be cautious of what may happen.

Even though almost everyone is talking about innovation, there is not much innovation happening. There are two major hindrances: "being mediocre" and "bound by precedents".

It was said, "the biggest enemy of success is not failure, but mediocrity." If you try and fail, you can always try again; if you accept mediocrity, you will never begin. Innovation is to try something new. A person being bound by precedents is against anything that has not been done before. It is certainly very safe to just copy what others have done before but it will not allow innovation to happen.

Germany invented many new bridge technologies in the course of rebuilding the country after the destruction of WWII. Orthotropic bridge deck, cable-stayed bridges, segmental construction, etc. contributed greatly to the advancement of bridge technology for the entire world. Those innovations were not without risks. True, bridge engineering is public work. It does not allow serious accidents. But, in the course of innovation, small accidents do happen. Still, we must continue to innovate. Engineering is not science. Engineering is based on experience and experience is never complete. The orthotropic deck is a good example. The concept of an orthotropic bridge deck has been applied to steel bridges for over 50 years now, but we still cannot claim to know everything about orthotropic bridge decks. Nevertheless, we continue to build bridges with orthotropic bridge decks and have been improving our knowledge about it along the way. This is because remedying a little error is acceptable. Just like the progress of China is based on what Mr. Deng Xiaoping had said: "To cross the river by touching the stones". We engineers should learn from that too!

Human beings are not machinery. During our lifetime, we may be affected by some not so rational ideas. For example, some people may believe such round numbers as 3,000 and 4,000 to be some sort of boundary. There is no difference between 2,999 and 3,000. They are just numbers. When the Golden Gate Bridge was being designed, it was not like what we see today because some people believed that a suspended span should not be over 1,000 meters. The shape of the Golden Gate Bridge became what we see today only after the George Washington Bridge was built with a main span over 1,000m.

Some people like to fight for being "Number 1". They spend large sums of money to build the longest span. Currently, the world's longest spans: the 330m span Shibanpo girder bridge, the 552m span Chaotianmen arch bridge, the 1,088m span Sutong cable-stayed bridge and the 1,991m span Akashi suspension bridge are far from what we can build today. The limitation on span length today is not defined by technology but by cost. Therefore, making a bridge span longer is not innovation. It does not create any value.

There has been a lot of discussion about whether China is now a big country or a strong country in bridge construction. Such discussion has little meaning. Whether we are strong or not depends on whether we can compete with other countries and win. If we can win, we are stronger. If we cannot win, then we are not. The basic requirement to win a competition depends heavily on our ability to innovate.

Huihai Road Bridge · Lianyungang, Jiangsu

The Huihai Road Bridge is a part of Huihai Road which is the main thoroughfare of the new town in Lianyungang, Jiangsu Province. The bridge is located near the center of the new central business district. Aesthetics was a very important design criterion. The total length of the bridge is 304m. The main span with the butterfly arches is 100m long. Construction of the bridge broke ground on August 10, 2010. It was opened to traffic on December 28, 2012.

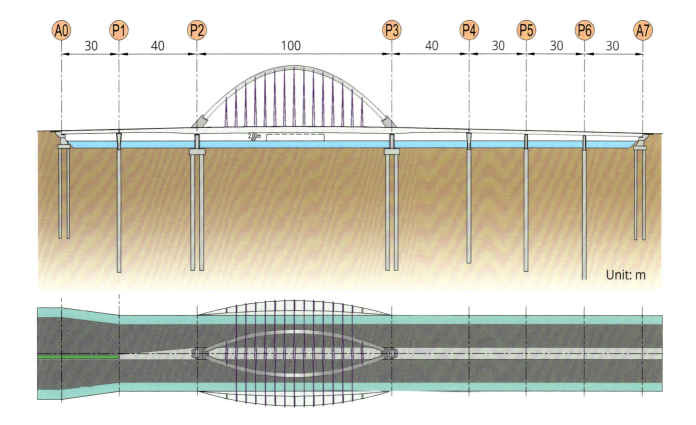

The Owner requested a signature bridge for the City. The prerequisite for being a signature bridge is that it must be beautiful and unique. I think the selected design satisfies this requirement!

We named it a "Butterfly Arch Bridge".

The 100m main span features a pair of connected tied arches that look like the wings of a butterfly. Each arch rib has two planes of hangers. The three-dimensional hanger arrangement prevents the arch ribs from lateral buckling. This allows the arch ribs to be more slender. The structural principle is similar to that of the Dagu Bridge in Tianjin except that both arch ribs are connected to the deck at the centerline of the bridge. A tie is placed underneath the arch and inside the concrete box girder. The force in the tie is slightly larger than the horizontal thrust of the arches so as to always have residue compression in the box girder. The arch ribs are trapezoidal steel boxes. The girder is a multi-cell, prestressed concrete box girder, which carries all torsional moment in the bridge created by unbalanced loadings. The arches carry only vertical loads. The arch ribs have a trapezoidal cross section. They express a stronger character.

Huihai Road Bridge · Lianyungang, Jiangsu

Huihai Road Bridge · Lianyungang, Jiangsu

When we conceptualize a bridge, we must ensure that it will look good from all different view points.

 The deck is 38m wide. The two arch ribs converge to the center line of the deck. Thus, the entire load of the bridge is supported by the piers at these locations.
 The bridge is designed based on the concept of a partially cable-supported girder bridge.

148 COMPOSING BRIDGES

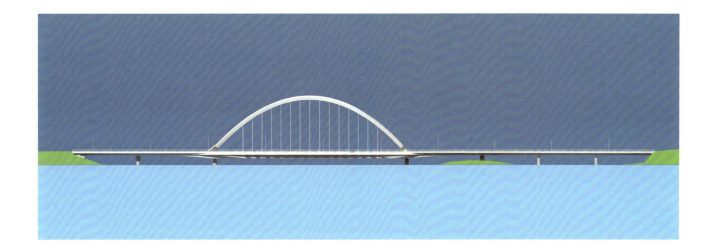

   Each arch rib has two planes of hangers. The outside hanger plane is pushed outward to provide sufficient vertical clearance to the traffic lanes and pedestrians.
   In the approach spans, the bridge is separated into two superstructures, with a 6m gap between them. Each superstructure carries three lanes of city traffic and a 5m-wide pedestrian/bicycle path.
   The total width of the deck is 5.0 + 11.5 + 6.0 + 11.5 + 5.0 = 39.0m.

The Art of Arches

The history of arch can be traced way before the Roman Empire. Early arches, such as the Ishtar Gate of Babylon, was built as early as 600 BC. However, the Romans really mastered the art of building arches. They built many spectacular arch bridges and viaducts, some of which are still standing after 2,000 years.

The arch is the oldest form of long-span bridges. The arch is the only bridge form that can carry loads using material with a very low tensile capacity, such as stones and bricks. That is why all long-span bridges in ancient time were arches. They did not have materials that could withstand tension at that time, such as steel or other metals. All Roman arches are stone arches. They are very heavy, which is beneficial too. It gives the arch the capability to resist lateral loads from wind, water and earthquake.

Modern arches are much lighter. They are mostly built using steel or reinforced concrete. These materials have tensile capacities. A modern arch rib using these modern materials can take both compression as well as bending moment, which implies possible tensile stresses in the cross section.

It is interesting to note that all Roman arches are basically semi-circular with the rise equal to the radius of the arch. The first long span non-semicircular arch appears to be the Anji Bridge in Zhaozhou, China, which has a span of 37m and a rise of 7m, resulting in a rise to span ratio of 1: 5.3, which is within the range of rise to span ratio of today's modern arch bridges.

Modern arches can have different shapes: besides the semicircular Roman arches, an arch can be partial circular like the Anji Bridge, or parabolic, elliptical, gothic or other combinations of shapes. Circular arch looks more conservative, its geometry is easier to develop. It was popular during the Renaissance period too but fell out of favor in the succeeding Baroque era. Personally, I like parabolic arch better. I think it is more graceful and lively. Almost all arch bridges I designed have parabolic shape, such as the Caiyuanba Bridge, Dagu Bridge, etc. Gothic arch is very tall and is more suitable for churches, which gives people a superhuman feeling. But it is too tall and is not practical for bridge construction.

An arch can carry heavy loads acting in its own plane. In the lateral or "out-of-plane" direction, however, modern arches are very flexible and cannot resist much lateral load. Further, because the main force in an arch rib is compression, an arch rib will be unstable and can buckle in the lateral direction unless it has a sufficiently high lateral stiffness. Lateral stiffness can be enhanced either by widening the arch rib to increase its lateral rigidity or by cross bracing two arch ribs against one another. The first method would make the arch look too bulky while the second method would be appropriate only for longer-span arch bridges.

For medium- to short-span arches, I prefer utilizing two planes of hangers to stabilize the arch, making it a three-dimensional structure. This way, the arch rib can be made very slender, as in the cases of the Dagu Bridge in Tianjin and the Huihai Road Bridge in Lianyungang. This creates three planes of forces—two hanger planes and the arch plane.

Both the Dagu Bridge and the Huihai Road Bridge have two arch ribs. The difference between these two bridges is that the Dagu Bridge arches are located apart from each other while for the Huihai Road Bridge the two arches converge to meet at one point at the deck level. Therefore, in the Dagu Bridge, the arches can resist all eccentric loads on the deck, whereas the Huihai Road Bridge must have a torsional rigid box girder to resist any eccentric load on the deck .

For short- to medium-span bridges, torsional moment due to an unbalanced load can be easily carried by a box girder, thus making it possible to use one single arch in the middle, or a converged double arch like the Huihai Road Bridge, or even just a single arch suspending the deck at one side only if the deck is a box girder.

Second Yangtze River Bridge
Changshou, Chongqing

The bridge has a main span of 739m and its ground-breaking ceremony was held on October 30, 2010. But actual construction did not start until December 25, 2017. It was opened to traffic on June 25, 2021.

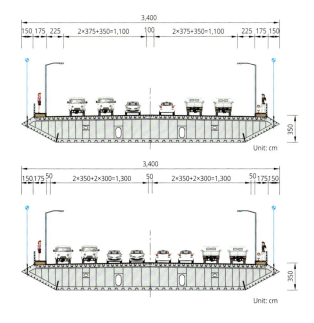

The Changshou Second Yangtze River Bridge crosses the Yangtze River in the southwestern area of the City. Its northern end connects with the main streets of the "Chemical Town" while its southern end is next to the Chongqing Steel Mill. There is an interchange at each end of the bridge. The total length of the project is 3,833m. The main bridge is 1,401m long with a suspension bridge main span of 739m. Only the main span is suspended. The landscape at both ends of the bridge is rather hilly. Since the hillside is very close to the bridge, suspending the end span would have made the bridge look messy.

The total width of the main girder is 34m including suspender anchorages. It has six traffic lanes but with sufficient width to expand to eight lanes in the future, if needed. Two pedestrian paths, one on each side, are 1.50m wide each. The suspended span is a 3.50m-deep, steel box girder. The deck is an orthotropic deck.

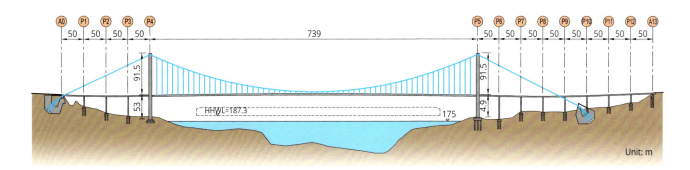

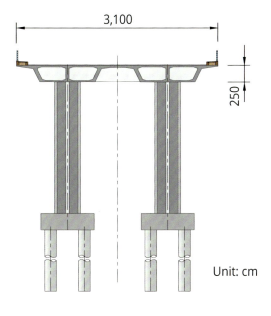

Considering that the bridge will be used by industrial vehicles and construction vehicles, the deck plate of the orthotropic deck has been thickened to at least 16mm to minimize possible damages that may be caused by overloaded trucks.

The approach spans are prestressed concrete box girders, 31m wide, 2.5m deep. Currently in China, steel box girders are about twice as expensive as prestressed concrete box girders. Using a prestressed concrete box girder for the approach spans reduces the cost of construction.

Both towers are located on land. This eliminates the danger of possible ship collision. The towers are constructed of concrete. They have a total height of 140m above the plinth and are about 90m above the bridge deck.

Second Yangtze River Bridge · Changshou, Chongqing

Changshou Second Yangtze River Bridge

Jialing River Bridge · Caijia, Chongqing

Caijia Jialing River Bridge carries Line #6 of the Chongqing Light Rail System. It crosses the Jialing River near the township of Caijia.

The bridge carries two tracks of light rail. The entire bridge project is 1,300m long. The main bridge is a five-span, continuous structure with span arrangement of 60 + 135 + 250 + 135 + 60 = 640m. The deck is about 110m above the normal water level.

Construction began on October 1, 2010. It was opened to traffic on December 1, 2013.

    The Jialing River Valley is a beautiful hilly landscape. It is very graceful and majestic. A bridge crossing at this location must be graceful and majestic too. We studied many bridge types and finally selected the concrete cable-stayed bridge for the final design. A two-track, light rail bridge is a rather skinny structure. Concrete offers more mass and a higher stiffness, which are good for both appearance and for damping bridge vibrations caused by the rail operations.

    I rejected all arch schemes because they were too imposing and difficult to build for a bridge that is high above the water. A suspension bridge would look nice, barring the anchorages. Suspension bridge anchorages are expensive and appear out of proportion for such a landscape. A self-anchored suspension bridge would not be economically feasible as well. The girder would have to be completed first before installation of the main cables and hangers.

A comparison of single- and double-plane cable-stayed bridge schemes

We studied a haunched box girder as one of the alternatives. But such a girder appears bulky. Besides, for rail operations, the requirement for the smoothness of the deck elevation is very stringent. As the creep and shrinkage behavior of a long-span, prestressed concrete box girders are still not fully understood, the long-term plastic deflection of a long-span concrete girder is difficult to predict. Even though long-term deflection of a concrete box girder can be compensated for by providing additional future post-tensioning, this is not very effective because the future tendons would have a very shallow profile running through the inside of the box girder. A cable-stayed bridge is better suited for future rehabilitation, if required. The cables, with their high profile, are much more effective. By providing some reserve in the design of the cables, any future cable force adjustment, if necessary, would be rather simple.

We have also studied the single-plane versus double-plane of cables. A single plane cable arrangement is workable because the girder is a box girder with sufficient torsional stiffness to carry the torsion created by the eccentric loading on the bridge. It may look better too. But the double-plane scheme was chosen by consensus.

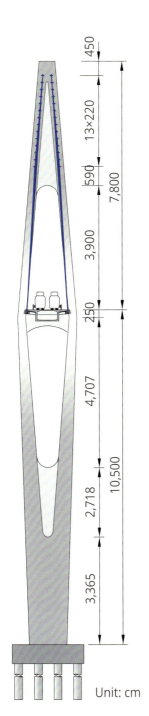

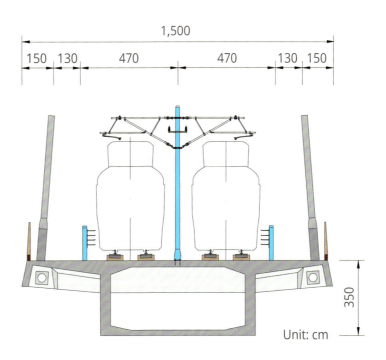

The girder is a prestressed concrete box girder, 15m wide and 3.5m deep. The deck is 105m above the top of the pile cap. The tower is diamond shaped. For such a tall and narrow tower, the diamond shape is especially suitable.

The water level of the Jialing River varies about 30m between high and low water seasons. So, we elongate the bottom solid portion of the tower to accommodate the variable water level. In this way the tower will look similar no matter what the water level is. This also offers a better protection against possible ship impact.

The girder is monolithically connected to the towers. This is possible because the lower portion of the towers is quite tall. This simplified the construction of the pier table.

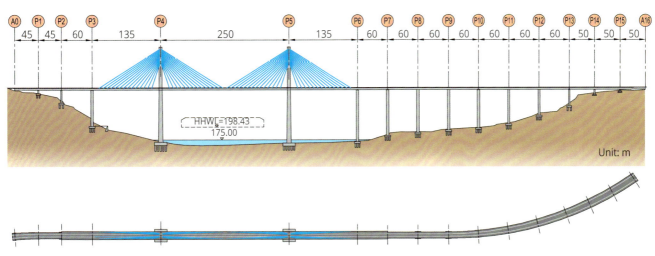

Jialing River Bridge · Caijia, Chongqing

Transit bridge over the Jialing River at Caijia

Single-plane and Double-plane Cable-Stayed Bridges

Some people may feel that a single-plane cable-stayed bridge is less reliable than a double plane cable-stayed bridge. In reality, many single-plane cable-stayed bridges have long been built and are still in operation.

The Stromsund Bridge in Sweden is usually recognized as the first cable-stayed bridge in the world. The bridge was designed by the German engineer Franz Dischinger. It has a 182m main span and was opened to traffic in 1955. That was 65 years ago. It has two planes of cables.

Original Nordelbe (1962)

Widened Nordelbe (1984)

Flehe (1979)

Neuenkamp (1971)

Brotonne (1977)

Early single-plane cable-stayed bridges

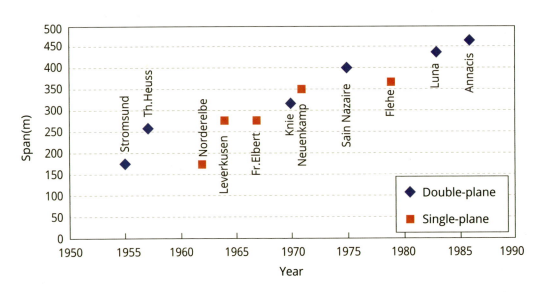

World records of single-plane and double-plane cable-stayed bridges

The first long span single-plane cable-stayed bridge is the Norderelbe Bridge in northern Germany. It was opened to traffic in 1962, seven years after the Stromsund Bridge. That was 58 years ago. The bridge has a main span of 172m and a deck width of 30.74m. Later, in 1984, the bridge was widened from four lanes to six lanes with some modifications to the cable spacing but remained as a single-plane cable-stayed bridge. In the meantime, the span of single-plane cable-stayed bridges got longer and longer. Both the Rhine Bridge at Leverkusen and the Rhine Bridge at Neuenkamp were the world's longest spans at the time they were opened to traffic—longer than all double-plane cable-stayed bridges at that time.

When concrete was still in its development stage, all long-span bridges were built by steel companies. Therefore, early long-span bridges including cable-stayed bridges were all steel bridges. The Hoechst Bridge over the Main River near Frankfurt, Germany is the first long-span concrete cable-stayed bridge. It was completed in 1972 with a 148m main span. This bridge carries six highway lanes, one railway track and a pipeline. It has two planes of cables spaced very close to each other, so they act more like a single cable plane. The 320m span, single-plane, concrete cable-stayed bridge, the Brotonne Bridge in France was completed in 1977. To date, the longest-span single-plane concrete cable-stayed bridge is the 420m span Second Bridge over the Panama Canal.

In the article *Single-plane Cable-Stayed Bridges Under Eccentric Loading* (M C Tang, Bridge Magazine, Beijing, April, 2010, in Chinese), I showed that the torsional stiffness of a 400m span single plane cable-stayed bridge with a box girder is actually higher than a double-plane, cable-stayed bridge with a plate girder. If a box girder is used, single-plane cable-stayed bridges are feasible.

Bridges Designed But Not Built

In several instances, a bridge was fully designed but was then placed on a waiting list due to changes in planning or a change of heart. The following are two such bridges. They are so special that I believe they deserve to be shown.

Guangli River Bridge · Dongying, Shandong

Dongying is a new city located on the east coast of Shandong Province. It has a large oil industry and is quite well off. The entire City is being built from scratch since the establishment of the oil industry. The lakes and canals are mostly manmade. The Guangli River Bridge is located on the Shengli Avenue which is the central axis of the City. The bridge is considered the Gateway to the City. At the other end of the avenue is the City government building. Aesthetics was a major consideration for the selection of a final bridge scheme.

Currently, there is an old bridge in the same location. The old bridge, a strut arch, is considered insufficient for today's traffic. A new bridge is to be built to replace the old bridge. As a matter of fact, the canal at that location will be enlarged so the original bridge must be replaced.

The government has tried to make the City more pleasant to live in. The City has contracted with several well-known architects to improve the cityscape and has built a spacious plaza in front of City Hall where citizens can gather to sing, dance, and enjoy many types of entertainment.

The bridge is located on the central axis of the City. At the other end, is the City Hall

As the central axis of the City, Shengli Avenue (*"Shengli" means "victory" in Chinese*) has been given special attention in its landscaping.

Guangli River Bridge, Dongying, Shandong

Guangli River Bridge · Dongying, Shandong

Development of a Gateway

a

b

c

d

e

A gateway can have many forms. Here is how I conceived the final configuration of this bridge:

Sketch a is like the Gateway Arch in St. Louis, Missouri, USA. The St. Louis arch is a huge stainless-steel arch. It is about 200m high—too high for our purposes. A smaller arch would be possible. But it would not inspire a great atmosphere like a large gateway would.

Sketch b is like the Arc de Triumph in Paris. It is nice but it is too bulky for this site.

After studying the sight line of a motorist who would drive through the gate into the City, I believed a door-type gate with a cross beam on top would not be suitable for this site because the cross beam obstructs one's sight and one must be close to the gate before he or she can see the buildings and scenes behind the gate. So, I decided that an open-type gate would look better.

Sketches c, d and e show the variations of an open-type gateway. Scheme c was discarded because it was not suitable for a bridge tower. Scheme d was good but it would have required a long and tall wall to reach a majestic scale. This would not look good from other angles in the area.

So, sketch e served as my basic idea for the bridge configuration. It can be made very majestic and it does not require an overpowering size.

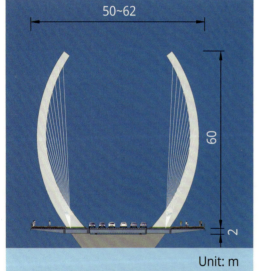

After settling on a basic scheme, the next step was to establish the proper size of the bridge. The river would be navigated only by pleasure boats that require small clearance. So, a main span of 90m was sufficient. This span length was chosen considering the size of the tower and the bridge's possible girder depth. A smaller span would not look good; a longer span would require a larger tower that is not proportional to the width of the bridge.

As a matter of fact, the height and cross section of the tower ribs, the deck width, and the span length are all related to one another. They must be treated as a single unit.

Obviously, the width of the bridge is determined by the cross section of the road on both ends of the bridge. In order to accommodate the tower ribs, I widened the deck near the tower slightly so that the pedestrian/bicycle paths curved a little outward. This provides a little more space for greenery on the bridge and it also increases the intrigue of the bridge.

Unit: m

168 COMPOSING BRIDGES

Because the bridge connects to the streets at both ends, the elevation of the deck is fixed. There is little room underneath the bridge. Hence a 2.00m depth was selected for the girder. The tower was placed in the water so that its reflection on the water would be a beautiful sight.

I inverted the cable arrangement, giving the bridge a beautiful twist. It is less efficient, but it looks really spectacular! For a bridge of this size, we can afford to lose some structural efficiency to gain in aesthetics.

It is important that a bridge must look good from all directions. Here are views of the bridge from various locations.

Color Schemes

It is very important to search for the best color combination for the structure. Here are the two finalists.

The red tower with golden cables is a very royal and conspicuous combination. It is majestic, befitting an emperor's palace. It seems a bit strong for an open space, as in our case.

Finally, we chose the white color combination. It will be more harmonious with the green water and the blue sky!

Dongping River Pedestrian Bridge
Foshan, Guangdong

The Dongping River Pedestrian Bridge connects two areas of a park divided by the Dongping River. The Owner indicated that aesthetics was the most important factor in the design competition. The proposed concept won first prize and was selected for final design.

The river traffic is very busy, so no pier was allowed in the river. Thus, the bridge had to span the entire river, resulting in a 305m span.

The new bridge is located adjacent to a highway bridge about 600m upstream. That bridge is an arch bridge. A stadium nearby is circular in plane view, therefore, a horizontally curved bridge fits best with this environment.

A curved bridge can have many forms. The sketch shows a few of the variations I studied during the conceptual design stage. As mentioned above, a single curve is preferable because it gives the feeling that the bridge is a single span across the river. It also fits better with the single-span arch bridge upstream. I placed the two towers, one on each side of the bridge. This looks good. In fact, under this arrangement, the force distribution in the girder is most efficient.

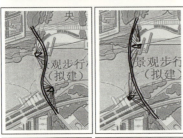

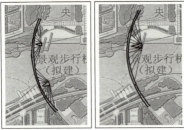

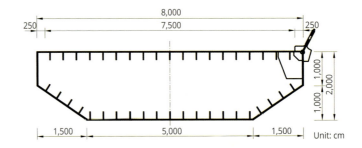

A box girder is inherently torsionally rigid. Due to this rigidity, we can build long-span box girders such as the Shibanpo Bridge with a main span of 330m. Even under the most unfavorable load conditions, there is hardly any noticeable rotation of the box girder. Consequently, we can use a one-sided cable arrangement for the Dongping River Pedestrian Bridge.

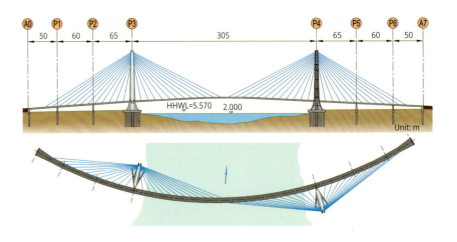

Rendering of the Dongping River Pedestrian Bridge

Stair and elevator are available to access the bridge from the ground level at the tower

Dongping River Pedestrian Bridge · Foshan, Guangdong

Simplified model test

8m-long full model test

Due to its rather non-traditional configuration and the spectacular size for a pedestrian bridge, we have carried out very extensive analytical and experimental studies to confirm its safety; this is not only for our requirements, but also necessary to convince the engineering community that the bridge is absolutely safe.

Before I proposed the concept for the design competition, I asked West Wind Laboratories in California to carry out a simplified wind tunnel test of a sectional model of the bridge. The result showed the bridge was very stable under the given design wind. During the final design stage, Tongji University performed a thorough aerodynamic study and again proved the bridge to be safe.

The design of the Dongping River Pedestrian Bridge took place not long after the Millennium Bridge in London was shut down right after its opening due to unacceptable oscillations caused by human-structure interaction. This phenomenon was also thoroughly studied for the Dongping River Pedestrian Bridge and found to be acceptable.

Some people were concerned with the rotation of the bridge deck under live loads because the box girder is supported by cables on one side only. Structural analysis showed that the maximum rotation of the deck would be less than 0.01 radian under the most unfavorable load distribution.

The towers are shell-like structures. Some people worried about buckling. Two analyses with different software found the safety factor against buckling to be over 9.00.

This bridge is very safe!

Night view of the Dongping River Pedestrian Bridge

Acknowledgement

Bridge design is teamwork. During the past 9 years in China, I have been very lucky to have had a team of excellent engineers working with me. I want to thank them for their hard work, their dedication and their enthusiasm. They are the main reason why we have achieved what we have achieved.

This team consists primarily of a group of young engineers; some of them joined us from other firms, but most of them joined T.Y. Lin International when they were freshly graduated from college. They worked hard, learned very fast, and are all high achievers. A few of them already have been promoted to managers of branch offices. The team is now led by Dr. Delan Yin.

Many from other offices of T.Y. Lin International, from San Francisco, Taipei, Singapore, and Kuala Lumpur, have also provided precious assistance, especially Dr. Tom Ho, Dr. John Sun, Chuck Seim, Michael Fitzpatrick, Rafael Manzanerez and Cheng Xu. These experienced engineers helped review the design and offered valuable advice and encouragement to young engineers.

I would also like to thank many of our engineers, especially the project managers of these bridges. They have been very helpful in reviewing the manuscript and have offered sound suggestions. The Photographic Society of T.Y. Lin, especially its President, Yaping Lai, kindly provided many of the pictures in this book.

Special thanks also to Pam Ching, who has kindly reviewed the manuscript and offered good suggestions.

Certainly, many of those outside of the company have also contributed significantly to the success of these projects, especially the owners, contractors, supervision teams, etc. I would like to thank them too, sincerely and collectively.

This book is an English translation from the Chinese edition by its author, Man-Chung Tang (邓文中). A few pictures were replaced by better ones.

The Chinese edition is called《造桥构思》, which was published in 2012, by Tsinghua University Press, Beijing, China.

Author: Man-Chung Tang (邓文中)

Dr.-Eng., Hon. Dr.-Eng., Hon. Dr. Lit., Hon. Architect, Hon. Professor, P.E.
Chairman of the Board, T.Y. Lin International
Structural engineer, specializes in bridges and special structures, has designed more than 100 major bridges
Member: National Academy of Engineering, USA
Foreign member: Chinese Academy of Engineering, PRC
Honorary Citizen: City of Chongqing, China

图书在版编目（CIP）数据

造桥构思 = Composing Bridges：英文 /（美）邓文中 (Man-Chung Tang) 著. — 北京：人民交通出版社股份有限公司, 2022.10
　　ISBN 978-7-114-17951-8

　　Ⅰ.①造⋯　Ⅱ.①邓⋯　Ⅲ.①桥梁设计—英文　Ⅳ.
①U442.5

中国版本图书馆 CIP 数据核字（2022）第 079061 号

著作权合同登记号　图字：01-2022-4484

Title: COMPOSING BRIDGES
An English Translation from the Chinese Edition
Author: MAN-CHUNG TANG（邓文中）
Editorial Production Manager: Zhu Mingzhou, Qu Tianshu
Proofreader: Sun Guojing, Song Jiashi
Printing Clerk: Liu Gaotong
Publisher: China Communications Press Co., Ltd.
Address: No.3, Waiguanxie Street, Chaoyang District, Beijing, 100011
Website: http://www.ccpcl.com.cn
Telephone: +86 (010)59757973
Chief Distributor: Sales Department of China Communications Press Co., Ltd.
Printer: Beijing Yinjiang Color Printing Co., Ltd.
Format: 635mm×965mm, 1/8 of a sheet
Sheets: 23
Word Counts: 405,000
Edition: First edition, Oct., 2022
Impression: First impression, Oct., 2022
Identifier: ISBN 978-7-114-17951-8
Price: ￥230.00
(The Press can replace books with printing or binding defects)